I Wonder:
Mind-Freeing
Encounters
with God

I Wonder: Mind-Freeing Encounters with God

Nathan Aaseng

CHRISTIAN ALTERNATIVE
BOOKS

Winchester, UK
Washington, USA

JOHN HUNT PUBLISHING

First published by Christian Alternative Books, 2021
Christian Alternative Books is an imprint of John Hunt Publishing Ltd.,
No. 3 East St., Alresford, Hampshire SO24 9EE, UK
office@jhpbooks.com
www.johnhuntpublishing.com
www.christian-alternative.com

For distributor details and how to order please visit the 'Ordering' section on our website.

ISBN: 978 1 78904 777 6
978 1 78904 778 3 (ebook)
Library of Congress Control Number: 2020947605

A CIP catalogue record for this book is available from the British Library.

Design: Stuart Davies

UK: Printed and bound by CPI Group (UK) Ltd, Croydon, CR0 4YY
Printed in North America by CPI GPS partners

We operate a distinctive and ethical publishing philosophy in all areas of our business, from our global network of authors to production and worldwide distribution.

Previous Nathan Aaseng books

Navajo Codetalkers 978-0802776273
Michael Jordan: Hall of Fame Basketball Superstar 978-1622850351
Killer Carnivorous Plants 9781978504332
Billy Graham 978-031039841
The Cold Flames 978-1446452369
You Are the Supreme Court Justice 978-1881568144
The Disease Fighters: The Nobel Prize in Medicine 978-0822506522
From Rags to Riches 978-0459572262
162 others

To my Dad, who opened the door to religious questions, to Linda, who has shared these questions with me, to my children, who were curious enough to read my sermons online after they left the house, and to all those who have honestly opened up to me with their questions during my ministry.

Introduction: Not Wonder?

The original ending of Mark's gospel has disturbed faithful Christians for centuries. Jesus does not even make an appearance in Mark's Easter story. All we have is hearsay evidence from an unnamed source, who nobody knows, that Jesus has risen from the dead. Mark's Gospel ends with this sentence, "So they went out and fled from the tomb, terror and amazement had seized them, and they said nothing to anyone, for they were afraid." End of story. That ending bothers Christians because it does not conclude with the requisite, ringing profession of unwavering faith. I have heard many attempts to explain this "unsatisfactory" ending to the very first of the gospels. But it was not until I pondered three separate experiences of confirmation students that it finally made sense to me.

I will never forget our oldest child coming home from confirmation class and relating what happened in class that day. He described how, during their second year of instruction, they were going over some doctrine that most of them had heard so many times they could have repeated it along with the pastor, assuming they could stay awake. One of them suddenly bolted upright in his seat at something the pastor had just said. His eyes wild with amazement and confusion, he blurted out, "Wait a minute! You mean Jesus was God's son?" At first, the class thought he was putting them on. How could you go through church and spend all that time in confirmation without hearing this? But he turned out to be one hundred percent sincere. Somehow, he had missed all the spoiler alerts in this well-worn tale, and he was absolutely blown away.

Now we can laugh at the kid's ignorance or shake our heads in despair over why he had not heard this bit of doctrine. But his reaction was right out of Mark's Gospel story. It was as genuine a reaction in our day and age as I have ever heard to the Easter

1

message—a story of love that is too astounding to comprehend. He did not say he believed it; he did not say he didn't believe. Like the folks in Mark's gospel, he had not gotten that far yet. He simply sat in utter, jaw-dropping wonder, so stunned that all he could say was, "Whoa!"

Compare that to a story I heard about another confirmation student, a boy who kept asking questions in class, such as where do the dinosaurs fit in with Genesis. The questions made those around him uncomfortable. After one of his queries, another student scolded him: "You're not supposed to wonder about things like that." To which the kid replied, "Not wonder? How can I help but wonder!"

As a third-career intern pastor, I encountered an entire class of students with his curiosity, only with attitude. Their stifled sense of wonder had turned to outright cynicism that dismayed their parents, pastors, and teachers. They challenged everything the church taught, and dismissed most of it. No one knew what to do with this bunch, and they certainly were not going to inflict them on an intern. But one evening, due to scheduling conflicts, I was assigned to fill in for an evening with this class. Amid a lot of belligerent and rude behavior, they began firing questions, challenges, and accusations at me so furiously and from so many angles, I felt like a goalie on a bad hockey team.

By grace or good fortune, the intended "victim" of their attack was a kindred spirit. I have always been the kid who could not help but wonder. Like Jacob of the Old Testament, I have often found myself wrestling with God, trying to make sense of the faith in which I have been raised. I throw everything I have at God—doubt, despair, questions. Through these encounters, my faith has grown deeper. The more I wrestle with God, the better I come to know God. In short, I was somewhat sympathetic to what I was hearing from these kids. Unlike a class that grudgingly, yet dutifully, puts in their time so they can get confirmed and please their parents or grandparents, these kids were real. They dared to pose questions that would get them closer to the truth, and rejected "answers" that did not really answer their questions. To their surprise, I applauded them and told them that those who never test their faith never know if any of it is true or not. Because of the questions they were asking, they had a good chance of discovering what was true.

After the kids got over their surprise, I was something of a hero to them. We finished the year with the best and deepest spiritual discussions I have ever had with any confirmation class. Members of that congregation could not believe the change in that group of kids. Ever since then, every confirmation class of mine devoted at least one session to asking questions and wondering.

I have often thought about the kid who was blown away by the Easter story and the kid who was told not to wonder. I wonder if either of them survived his experience of the faith community with that gift of wonder still intact, or whether it was eventually beaten out of him by the "God said it. I believe it. That settles it" defenders of the faith. I have often wondered how many thousands of people were deprived of a meaningful relationship with God because the medieval church insisted that Christian faith required a belief that the sun revolves around the earth, and that any wondering about that premise could get you excommunicated or even killed. When science proved that belief wrong, the natural conclusion for many was that Christianity is misguided superstition.

You would think Christians could have learned from that mistake. Yet many faithful members of congregations today are uncomfortable with, if not embarrassed by, some aspects of the Christian religion. They do not vocalize this because they understand they are not supposed to question religious teachings. They are not supposed to wonder.

Many of those raised in a church environment no longer have any active involvement with a church. They maintain a vague belief in God and possibly even in Jesus Christ, but view the church as an institution that fears the truth, that stifles faith with outdated rituals, doctrine, traditions, and superstitions, and so how can they trust anything they are taught? Increasingly, they see the church as an institution that refuses to meet them where they are or to listen to the questions they have. Instead, they hear the religious professionals saying, "Here are the questions you should be asking, and here are the answers." No wondering allowed.

At the same time, the number of agnostics and atheists in this country is growing rapidly, as many educated secular people find what is presented to them as Christianity to be ridiculous, largely because they have lost their sense of wonder. No sense that the very laws of nature are essentially arbitrary—magic that can be understood, ordered and catalogued. Believing that faith equals superstition, they choose reason and dismiss faith out of hand. No sense of wonder there either.

My experiences with young people, frustrated ex-Christians and the unchurched have caused me to ask why we continue to discredit Christianity by buying into that false equation and forcing people to make an artificial choice that removes all sense of wonder. This book is another of my rebellions against that false equation because, like that confirmation student, I can't help but wonder.

Those with a sense of awe and wonder about creation understand that it's a good idea to take off your shoes in the presence of the Almighty. But there's nothing about Christianity that requires you to check your brain or your curiosity at the door as well. Proverbs insists, in fact, that knowledge and wisdom are essential elements of faith. Absent those things, faith so easily dissolves into superstition, bland resignation, nostalgic habits, or disbelief. When that happens, there is no wonder, no mystery, no room for the Spirit to move and do all the creative, life-changing, world-changing things the Spirit can do.

I believe God gave us wonder and curiosity and reason, not as obstacles to faith, but as ways to know God better. This is hardly some New Age whim; it is deeply embedded in the Christian faith tradition. When asked by the church to renounce his heretical teachings, which had been spawned by daring to wonder, Martin Luther replied, "Unless I can be convinced by Scripture and plain reason, I cannot recant."

Nor should any of us. I wonder if that wasn't what the Gospel of Mark was meant to do: to put us in the shoes of the women at the tomb, or the disciples hearing this report, or any person hearing this incredible story of God's love and a triumph over evil for the first time. Or in the shoes of the confirmation student who awoke to that shocking claim about who Jesus is.

For them there was nothing routine or traditional about this story. Hearing it made the women and the disciples stop and say, "Wait a minute! You are saying Jesus rose from the dead! Whoa!"

Of course Mark's readers want to know what happened next. Mark says, don't be in such a hurry. Bask in the amazement. Live in the wonder. Feel what it is like to experience something so out of this world awesome that it leaves you trembling in confusion and fear, unable to speak. Let something that defies understanding sink in. Let the magic and the mystery of what you have heard wash over you. For just a few moments, don't say that you believe it. Don't say you don't believe it. Just sit there in stunned amazement at this incredible, stupefying story of a being powerful beyond our understanding whose love for us is beyond comprehension. Only after you've done that, do you try to put the pieces together and figure out what this story means for you and your life.

The first step in faith formation, as in science, is to wonder. To say, "Whoa!" To splutter out questions that beg to be asked. To eliminate our prepackaged, defensive, prideful explanations of what God is doing. The sooner we do that, the sooner we can get to the truth of that incredible love that God pours out upon God's creation, upon all of us.

Part I

Questions about God's Nature

Chapter 1

I Wonder:
If God is real, why doesn't God make it obvious and prove it once and for all?

This chapter is brought to you by Powdermilk biscuits. Heavens, they're tasty! They give shy people the strength to get up and do what needs to be done.

As a shy person, I've sometimes wished there were such a product as the fictitious sponsor of *A Prairie Home Companion*. There is a verse from John 17 that raises the issue of whether God is in need of some Powdermilk biscuits. "Righteous Father, though the world does not know you, I know you," declares Jesus. In the space of three verses, Jesus stresses the importance of making God known, and talks about how he is going to make God known to the world. This leads me to wonder: why doesn't God do it?

Doesn't this remind you of a common theme in literature—the shy guy who's in love with a woman but cannot bring himself to confront her? In *Cyrano de Bergerac, The Courtship of Miles Standish*, the motion picture *Roxanne*, and many other stories, the shy guy recruits an outgoing, more dashing, more assertive friend to make his presence known. The friend pleads his case while the shy guy lies back in the weeds and hopes for the best.

In the case of God, though, this shy behavior is bewildering. For centuries, people have been asking God, why don't you make yourself known? Why don't you get up and do what needs to be done? Why clutter the works with unreliable, highly flawed middle men, with easily missed and misinterpreted signs and intermediaries, and the mysteries of religious doctrine?

This business about believing or not believing in God seems such a waste of time and energy. *You, God, are supposed to be the powerful creator of the universe. If you want us to know you and believe in you, and honor and obey you, the solution is simple. Show up! Make an appearance! Step out where we can see you in all your glory. Dazzle us with your blinding light and your incredible power. Maybe knock a few heads together if you have to.*

You know that Damascus Road blinding vision thing that turned around the Apostle Paul's life? Just do that to everyone; that will make yourself known and then there will be no more division. No more religious squabbles. No more chasing after false gods. You will get that unity that Jesus prayed for. You will get those visions of glory and harmony that we read about in Isaiah and Revelation. It's so simple! Come on out. Don't be shy. Make yourself known.

If these thoughts have ever crossed your mind, you are not alone and you are not a bad person. Well, I suppose you could be, but not because of that! These wonderings are all over the Old Testament. Way back in Exodus, Moses asked the simple question of God: "What is your name?" As in, "Tell me a little about yourself."

God's response: "I am who I am," or "I will be who I will be."

Yeah, thanks for sharing. Based on this exchange, it seems maybe God isn't so good at relationships and *could* use a more socially adept middle man to get things going.

There is more discussion of this reclusive behavior later in Exodus, when we read that one of the basic rules of divine engagement is: God's face must not be seen. God must remain hidden. Over time, this shyness drives the Israelites crazy. "Why do you hide your face?" Job asks. The Psalmists line up one after another to ask the same thing:

Psalm 10: *Why do you hide yourself in times of trouble?*

Psalm 13: *How long will you hide your face from me?*

Psalm 27: *Do not hide your face from me.* And so on.

God's people pay a price for this shy behavior. Look at all the unbelievers who mock them for believing in a God who never shows up:

Psalm 42: *Where is your God?*

Micah 10: *Where is the Lord your God?*

Joel 2: *Why should they say among the peoples, where is your God?*
And so on.

It continues on into the New Testament. In Matthew, the magi come looking for Jesus, saying, "Where is the one who has been born king of the Jews?" No one seems to know anything about it. Why does this have to be such a secret?

In Matthew 6, Jesus advises the disciples to "pray to your Father who is unseen." Why is God unseen?

In Romans, Paul has to talk about God's invisible qualities. Why are these qualities invisible? In Mark, Jesus repeatedly orders those who understand that he is closely connected with God in a special way not to tell anyone about it. Why the request to remain anonymous?

The problem of God's shyness continues to puzzle us today. How many times have you longed for assurance from God, a little more clarity? How many people on that fateful day of September 11, 2001, or in the middle of the COVID-19 onslaught asked that same age-old question: where is God? How many of us, upon suffering a tragedy or crushing setback, ask with the Psalmist, "God, if you are there, why do you hide your face from me?" How many people trapped in the downward spiral of despair have been on their knees begging God to make an appearance? How many people have mocked the religious for naively calling on a God who shows no signs of being there.

If the goal, as Jesus says, is to make God known, does any of this make any sense? If God wants to be known, then why does God hide? Why disappear behind a cloak of invisibility and teasingly pass out such meager hints as can be found in our struggles to interpret an old and often baffling collection of inspired books, or in the occasional paranormal revelation? This is shy person behavior. It makes me wonder: could it be that God is, by nature, painfully shy? That sounds bizarre, and perhaps even disrespectful, but as long as we're wondering, let's explore the possibility that it is true.

There actually is a research center known as The Shyness Institute, located in Palo Alto, California. According to these people, about 50% of the population describe themselves as shy, up 10% from previous decades. Only 5% of people claim they are never shy. In other words, some degree of shyness is almost universal.

The Shyness Institute gives three definitions of shyness:

1. excessive self-consciousness
2. excessive negative self-evaluation
3. excessive negative self-preoccupation

I can't imagine how God could be any of these:* God is the antithesis of self-consciousness and self-preoccupation.* While in Old Testament stories God is sometimes said to have regrets about the role given to humans, it is silly to imagine God feels unworthy of conversation or relationship with the people God created. God is the essence of sharing, of giving, of concern for others. If shyness is simply a debilitating condition of low self-esteem that prevents us from interacting with others, there is no way God can be shy.

But as a shy person, I reject the prevailing idea that my shyness is simply a debilitating character flaw. There is another aspect to shyness that well-meaning extroverts fail to understand, and that is the reluctance to impose one's self on others. Not because of any feelings of unworthiness, but simply out of respect. Honestly, one of the roots of my shyness is that I live in dire fear of boring you.

Shyness can be a useful inhibition, an instinctive way of protecting another person's right to respond and relate free of coercion. It can actually be a selfless action that runs counter to the "look out for number one" syndrome that leads to so much conflict. That type of shyness actually makes sense to me as a characteristic of God, for this reason: It seems that what God desires most is shared relationship. True relationship cannot be accomplished in the absence of freedom. It cannot be demanded or coerced. God is well aware of the massive power differential between God and the rest of us. If confronted with the full force of that power and majesty, every person on earth would be cowed into submission. We would have no choice but to submit to whatever God said to do. And how do you get love out of that situation?

The Israelites explained God's "shyness" by saying that God's presence was so intensely, overwhelmingly brilliant that no one could survive in that presence. For years I thought that meant that any mere mortal who drew too near God would be physically incinerated by God's holy, blinding aura. That has never made sense to me. Surely God is capable of assuming a form that is not lethal to humans. But now, when I put this in the context of relationship, I wonder if the Hebrews were right. I have known couples where one person has such a powerful personality that it seems as if his or her partner disappears when the two of them are together. If God were to appear in all of God's brilliance and power, we would be so overwhelmed that we would absolutely disappear from the relationship. If that is the case, then the bravest, most extreme move God ever made was to put at risk the entire creation by assuming the shyness that makes true relationship possible. That gamble is the ultimate gift of love.

God loses this outrageous gamble many times. Jesus was speaking the truth when he said much of the world does not know God, does not recognize anything of great value in the unseen God. Like small children, we are wowed by flash and sizzle, and scared by thunder. The world obeys power, but it doesn't love it. But what if God loves us so much that God is willing to take a chance on being rejected, ignored, mocked, tamed, and repackaged in our own image, so that our relationship has a chance of being true? So that the love we return to God is not coerced but freely given.

This would require a delicate balancing act. God stays back in the shadows where we cannot see God's face. God's invitation comes through intermediaries. Sure, God could win converts by riding through the sky on a gigantic, blazing, winged horse, bellowing with the voice of thunder. God could wow us by making giant waffles dance in the street. But it is not God's power that God wants to impress upon us. God is looking for something deeper and more mature. And so, God is content to become known not through awesome acts of overwhelming majesty, but through intermediaries. Through the life of Jesus. Through the apostles. Through ordinary folk.

These intermediaries are not going to blow us away or sweep us off our feet. They are not going to make us cringe in terror and bow before the power that could crush us like a bug. If they are following in Jesus' footsteps, they will simply proclaim the quiet, solid truth that a world is coming in which tears and sorrow are no more, and that God would like nothing better than to share that world with us.

"The Lord is known by his justice," says Psalm 9. And God is known by God's love, says the whole story of the life and death and resurrection of Jesus.

Maybe that is as much as we are able to know about God without being coerced by God's brilliance into an empty relationship. If we see what God is all about, minus the sizzle and fireworks, and find that we want to return God's love, then the risk will have been worth it. If that is what's behind the veil of shyness, I understand it as a privilege to be the intermediary, the one who takes this message to the next person on behalf of the God of love and justice who stands in the shadows.

Chapter 2

I Wonder:
Why doesn't God give clear answers to our questions?

On Thanksgiving a number of years ago, we had a big family get-together at our house. I asked my dad if he would offer the prayer before the meal. As he started his prayer, I had second thoughts about having asked him. He began talking about those who did not have, about those who have far less than we do for which to be thankful.

While I knew every word he spoke was true, I could not help but wonder if this was really the time and the place for that kind of attitude. Thanksgiving is supposed to be a feast of gratitude for the bounty of creation, a celebration of God's generosity, a time of joy. What he said did not make me feel at all joyful. I wondered, is this a peculiar quirk of religious folks? Do we have to dampen all of our celebrations with an industrial strength load of guilt?

I found support for my complaint in the book of Ecclesiastes: *To everything there is a season, and a time for every purpose under heaven* — a time to weep, and a time to laugh. There is a time to confront injustice in the world, and a time to give thanks. Why do we mix them up? Have you ever seen a birth announcement that includes a somber statement of sympathy for those who may have lost loved ones today? Do we interrupt our Fourth of July fireworks for a vigil of silence for all those countries that do not enjoy the freedom and prosperity that we do? During a wedding banquet or a romantic Valentine's dinner, do we pause to remember those who have been unlucky in love? Of course not! Then why do it during Thanksgiving, I wondered. What's the point in having a celebration if you're not going to celebrate?

Those thoughts started spinning through my mind again as I came across a lectionary set of Advent Scripture readings. My first reaction was that whoever put this selection of readings together had to have been on some kind of mind-altering drug. Either that or they were trying to dream up the ultimate brain-teaser for preachers.

Zephaniah presented an upbeat message: "Sing aloud ... shout ... rejoice ... have no fear ... I shall restore your fortunes before your eyes." Ah, I like where this is going. Move on to Philippians: "Rejoice! Have no anxiety about anything. The peace of God that passes all understanding will keep your hearts and minds in Christ Jesus." Yes, I like this! I see a sermon coming together: redemption, joy, and celebration. Let's see what Luke has to add to the party and we'll be all set to go: "You brood of vipers! Flee from the wrath that is to come. Even now the axe is laid to the root of the tree: every tree that does not bear good fruit is cut down and thrown into the fire. His winnowing fork is in his hand to gather the wheat, but the chaff he will burn with unquenchable ..." Aw, come on! How can I proclaim both of these at once? The Lord is coming to bring peace to quiet your hearts, you brood of vipers, and he's comin' with an axe! Have no anxiety about anything with the small exception of that winnowing fork and the unquenchable fire of hell that's staring you in the face.

Hey, listen to Ecclesiastes: there's time and a season for everything. Let's not mix them up. But then my complaints echoed back to me when I reflected on what had just taken place at church in our Advent preparations. One week we were sorting out the Scriptural warnings and the sobering consequences of a life of sin, and the next week we bounced back to the children and their wonderfully upbeat Christmas program. And I had to wonder, "Is Advent the season we all go crazy and ride a wild rollercoaster of emotions? And is this any way to prepare for Christmas?" Well, maybe it is. That notion came to me from the most unlikely of places—a funeral. Have you ever experienced this, where someone steps up to deliver a eulogy and tells an absolutely hilarious story about the departed that has the sanctuary roaring with laughter? And a few minutes later a soloist walks to almost the exact spot, and halfway through a beautiful piece, breaks down in sobs and struggles to finish?

It was a profound moment when I first saw that happen. Helpless laughter and crushing grief spilled into each other. Totally different moods, opposite reactions to the situation. And do you know what? Both were entirely appropriate. Both were fitting tributes to the memory of the deceased.

It put me in mind of a book by E. F. Schumacher called *Small Is Beautiful*. Schumacher argues that the essence of what it means to be human is to engage in the struggle to reconcile the irreconcilable. What this means is that the human struggle boils down to somehow finding our way between totally opposite poles, both of which are true.

Schumacher explains it this way. So many people think that the goal of human life is to find the answers. We're all looking for the answers, and if only we could find the answers we would have life by the tail. No, says Schumacher. If you discovered all the answers about how to live your life, you would not be alive. You see, there *are* those in this world who know everything they are supposed to do, down to the last detail, in the exact order they are supposed to do them. We call them computers, robots, cyborgs. They function very well, very efficiently. But they are not truly alive. For humans, being alive means wrestling every day with questions that have no answers. Living between opposites.

Freedom and responsibility are total opposites. Yet we need both in our lives. How do you hold them together? How do you live with both burning passion and objective detachment? How do you fight evil while living a life of peace?

Love and justice
Law and Gospel

Change and preservation
Flexibility and steadfastness
Courage and prudence
Individuality and community
Rationality and feelings

There are no answers to the paradoxes that these opposites pose, there is only trying to find our way between them.

To most of us, that's frightening. We would rather skip the struggle and go back to the quest for answers, preferably easy answers as if *All I Ever Really Needed to Know I Learned in Kindergarten*. That's why one of the most popular genres of nonfiction is the How-To book. Books that have all the answers. Demographic studies show that in the past 40 years, the church denominations that have grown the fastest are the ones that claim to have all the answers. The ones who claim that Scripture is an instruction manual written by God himself that contains black-and-white answers to everything. In the twenty-first century we are so exhausted by the demands of an ever-changing, fast-paced world that we want to just hang it up. We desperately seek programming instructions so that we can avoid the headache of having to actually live our lives. Strange, isn't it? As our machines grow in complexity, we seek escape from complexity, and the result is that machines and humans grow more alike each day. I wonder, will the day come when we are so scared of life that we won't be able to tell machines and humans apart?

There was a time when I wondered why God doesn't give clear answers to all the questions of life. This has nothing to do with the shyness wondered about earlier. Surely God could let us know exactly what we are to do while remaining in the shadows.

Thanks to Schumacher, and the curious selection of lectionary readings, I have started to suspect that answers are not where it's at. Why are we so dead-set on seeking programming instructions for our so-called lives rather than learning the art of living? Why don't we focus on what life is all about? Why don't we focus on learning how to steer a course between the incompatible truths of freedom and responsibility, between love and justice, between Law and Gospel, between joy and sorrow?

We see all Christian churches everywhere struggle with the worship wars between contemporary and traditional. So much energy is expended on trying to find the best way to worship. Every congregation is looking for the correct answer. Well, surprise, surprise, no one has found it. Congregations either roll the dice on one style or the other, or else throw their hands up in despair over the intractable worship wars that rage in pretty much every congregation. Of course that's what happens, because finding the answer is a dead-end approach. There are no definitive answers to the worship dilemma—there is only the faithful struggle to steer between the opposite truths of maintaining the tradition that nurtures us, and adapting worship to the context in which we live.

I wonder what is it about life that scares us so badly. Does the gift of life terrify us because it is a gift that is huge, beyond our imagination? It seems to be more than we can handle. It's a gift that we try time and again to return to sender, or exchange it for the safer, more sensible gift of programming instructions. But life is a gift God wants us to have, and so every time I try to cash it in for a ride on the robot circuit, God keeps giving it back to me. God gives life to us along with the guiding principles, such as the commandments, the prophets, the Sermon on the Mount, the letters of Paul, that help us to steer well enough to stay on the road between these opposites. God shines the light of grace in front of us at all times, so that we can get a better view of the road as we try to steer between the opposite realities of life. God restores us with forgiveness when we veer off the road.

That's all good training for life. But most of all, God equips us with faith and love, and with the promise that the road will be worth traveling. Faith, love, and the promises of God give me the courage to keep going rather than taking the easy way out of pulling off the road and giving up on life.

I'm still not entirely sold on Dad's prayer. My Thanksgiving prayer ends up being a little different than his. But that does not mean that my prayer is the right one—because there is no right answer to how to give a Thanksgiving prayer. There is only the faithful struggle with the gift of life. And I can now accept Dad's heart-felt prayer gratefully as his faithful attempt to find his way between opposites in the light of God's redeeming grace.

"I come to bring you life that you may have it more abundantly," said Jesus. Have you ever noticed he's constantly telling people not to be afraid? I wonder if he means, "Do not be afraid of this gift of life. Don't turn away from life and settle for robotic existence. Enjoy the gift of life to its fullest."

So, here's a proposal: Instead of looking to religion for answers, maybe we should look to religion to help us steer. Maybe resistance exercises like these will help us learn to live:

1. Let's get on our knees before God and ask forgiveness ... and stand up tall and proud, singing with the angels, "Glory to God in the highest!"

2. Let's shed a tear for someone we miss ... and let our houses shake with laughter as friends and family gather.

3. Let's spend some time in quiet reflection ... and get out there and fight for what we know is right.

4. Let's fear the power of evil ... and celebrate the gentle love that descended upon the earth at Christmas.

5. Let's say a prayer for someone in need ... and give thanks to the Lord, for he is good and his mercy endures forever.

Let's struggle with our questions and doubts. While we enjoy the peace of God that passes all understanding.

Chapter 3

I Wonder:
Does God really know everything that is going to happen?

I ran across this story from a guy who swears it's true:

A pastor discovered a cat stuck high in a tree in his backyard. He tried everything to coax the animal down, including a saucer of milk. Nothing worked. The tree, although tall, was not very sturdy and so there was no chance of climbing all the way to the top to rescue the cat.

After mulling over the situation, the pastor attached a rope about halfway up the tree and tied the other end to his pickup truck. His plan was to slowly bend the tree until the top was close enough to the ground that he could reach the cat.

Slowly, carefully, he eased the truck forward, checking every few feet on his progress as the tree bent lower. He nearly got the cat within reach when the rope broke. The tree snapped back in place with tremendous force. As the pastor looked on in horror, the cat sailed high into the sky and clear out of sight.

He raced in the direction that the cat flew, hoping to recover it, if indeed it was still alive. But he could find no evidence of it. All week long he was racked with guilt for what he had done to the poor, frightened animal.

While shopping at the grocery store at the end of the week, he ran into one of his parishioners, who was loading some cat food into her cart. Knowing that the woman had always hated cats, he asked her what she was doing.

"Well, pastor," she said. "My daughter has been begging for a cat and I told her absolutely not. She kept begging so hard that I finally said, 'The only way you're getting a cat is if God himself delivers it.'" Instead of ending the matter, the girl took that as a hopeful sign and began praying for God to send her a cat. "Sure enough, last Monday I was out in the backyard with her when this cat flew into the yard right out of the sky. Hey, if God wants that badly for her to have a cat, who am I to take it away from her?"

Alright, I'm skeptical about this story, but I know strange things happen in this world. For argument's sake, let's accept the story as told. It brings up an interesting theological discussion: what does God control, and what does God know? There are two standard answers to these questions:

1. God controls everything that happens in this world.

That is basically the claim of predestination. God not only knows everything that will happen before it happens, but has actually arranged for things to happen as they do. God planned your life for you down to the smallest detail long before you were born. Advocates of this view cite Psalm 139:16 "All the days ordained for me were written in your book before one of them came to be."

I don't have a lot of patience for that kind of thinking. Looking at this story, according to this view, God decided many centuries ago that at this moment in time, he would coax a cat into a tree, gave a pastor the crazy idea to hook up the ropes to a truck, then cut loose the rope so the cat would go flying across the town into the yard of this little girl who was praying for God to send her a cat.

Anyone who would purposely do something like that to a cat is weird, and has a warped sense of humor. I see nothing in the Bible to suggest that God is like that.

2. While God does not control everything that happens because of the gift of free will, God knows everything that will happen.

Scriptural backing for this, oddly enough, comes from one verse before the previous one I quoted: verse 15 of Psalm 139: "When

I was woven together in the depths of the earth, your eyes saw my unformed body." This seems to be the majority Christian view at the moment. According to this, God was well aware that the girl would ask for a cat, and may even have exercised some influence to make sure that she got one. But most of the details just happened by chance, in just the way God knew they would happen. I can sympathize with this view because we have often been taught that God is omniscient, God knows everything. But if I accept this premise, it makes me feel sorry for God, and I cannot imagine God is a person who wants, or needs, or in any way deserves my pity.

Suppose it *were* true that God knows everything that is going to happen. What a dull, joyless existence! Imagine a life without any drama, in which everything plays out according to a script that you memorize well ahead of time. No spontaneity, no surprise. In our world, we call that living in a rut. I'm looking for something that makes more sense, which makes me intrigued by Bible verses that show a very different understanding of God. Unlike the other two views, they are not cherry-picked verses of poetry taken out of context, but rather represent a consistent theme found throughout the Bible. This view is that God can be, and often is, totally surprised by what happens in the world. According to this view, God may have been as surprised as anyone to see a cat flying through air into some little girl's yard.

There's that passage from Exodus in which the Israelites have turned away from the God who freed them from slavery in Egypt. They have built and worshipped an idol in the form of a golden calf. God is furious at their betrayal. "I have seen these people," says the Lord to Moses, "and they are a stiff-necked people. Now leave me alone so that my anger may burn against them and I may destroy them." God has made a decision. These people are toast. They had their chances and they blew them all. God had a plan and put forth a great effort to make it work, but the Israelites wrecked it because they refused to cooperate. God sees no further reason to continue this failed experiment, but will go on to try something new.

What happens next? After Moses presents his case, we are told, "the Lord relented and did not bring on his people the disaster he had threatened." The Hebrew word used here can be interpreted as relented or repented. Or as the NRSV translation says, "God changed God's mind." Moses talks God out of this plan! This is not the story of a God who controls everything or knows everything that is going to happen. It is not a script where everyone plays the parts that God assigned to them. God didn't even know what God was going to do. If you really want to spend some time down the rabbit hole, try imagining that God knew that God was going to change God's mind. Or even that God foreordained that God would change God's mind. The absurdity is too much for me.

It makes more sense to understand this as the story of a God who sought relationship and voluntarily set aside a certain amount of power in order to achieve it. This is a story of a God who sought a way to save a lost people from their destructive existence, and was greatly upset when people refused to cooperate. God was looking for a reason to continue with the plan of saving people by forming a covenant with them, but could not find it. From God's point of view, it looked hopeless, and God saw no choice but to turn to other options ... until Moses gave God the reason that God sought. It's not that Moses was smarter than God and came up with a better idea. Rather, through his own testimony of faith, Moses showed that while the plan to save humankind may fail with a lot of people, it is not hopeless. There *are* faithful people who try to cling to the promises, and to enter into the full life that God desires for all people.

An angry, disappointed God was pleasantly surprised by that. This faith of Moses was something new to be factored in, something that God had hoped for but had not expected. If God had known that was going to happen, God would not have made that idle threat to destroy the Israelites. Now that this has come to pass, God reevaluates the new situation, and changes God's mind.

I have to admit that I really wonder about those who cherry-picked isolated verses, stories, and incidents and turn them into absolute laws about what we should do and believe. So, I have to ask, is this episode with Moses just an isolated story that lies outside the core of what the Bible teaches? No, it seems to be a common theme, one that again shows up clearly in the two parables from Luke having to do with lost items: lost sheep and a lost coin. Jesus talks about the joy that results when the lost are found. "There will be more rejoicing in heaven over one sinner who repents than over 99 righteous who do not need to repent."

Joy is an emotion far more intense than contentment or happiness. The intensity of joy comes from the element of surprise or relief. Joy does not happen over the expected; it happens over the unexpected. Joy happens over the hoped for, but not sure it's going to happen.

Football fans who watch their team destroy a cupcake opponent 66–0 may be pleased or content with the result, but they but do not rush the field and tear down the goalposts when it's over. They are not beside themselves with joy. Compare that to the reaction of fans at Pittsburgh during a famous playoff game against the Oakland Raiders. On the last play of the game, the Steelers trailed and were far from the end zone with virtually no chance of winning. Their last desperate pass was batted down by the Oakland safety. Game over. Massive disappointment. Except that, miraculously, the ball was scooped up by Pittsburgh running back Franco Harris just before it hit the ground, and he ran into the end zone for a game-winning score. Absolute pandemonium broke out. Steeler fans were screaming, jumping, falling over, howling with delight.

The difference between the scenarios is the surprise factor. Everyone believed this game to be over. Steelers fans expected a loss. Suddenly, the unexpected happens, and the loss turns into a win. Now you have joy. When a lost person is saved according to a script that God knew would unfold, you might expect God to be pleased or content. But the emotion described throughout the passage in Luke is joy. Joy happens when despite the odds, despite the dangers and the fears of what could go wrong and probably will, the lost person is saved.

A German movie called *The Tunnel* is a wonderful illustration of the God presented to us by Jesus in these parables. It is based on the true story of a German swimmer who found himself and his sister trapped in East Berlin when the infamous wall went up in the early 1960s. The swimmer manages to escape and then dedicates his life to getting his sister and other people out. He recruits a group of people who all have the same goal—to somehow bring their loved ones out of East Berlin and into freedom. Using only picks and shovels, they begin to dig a tunnel from a basement in a West Berlin building—a tunnel that goes deep under the wall, avoids all detection, and comes up in an abandoned building on the other side. Their plan is to gather all their loved ones to that spot at just the right time, and bring them out.

The task seems hopeless, but this swimmer is relentless. He digs and he digs and he digs. His will to save his sister is so strong that he simply will never give up, and this iron will and the blood, sweat, and tears that he spends in this process inspires those around him. He and his friends develop a network inside East Germany that makes contact with all the people they plan to save, and design a plan to put them in the right place to make it all happen. Despite this incredible effort, the odds against them are enormous. East German security is active and vigilant and becomes aware of this group and what they are trying to do. It is an intense, nerve-wracking story. (Spoiler alert!) Not everyone is saved. But some are. And the scene at the end of the movie is the epitome of the joyful celebration in heaven that Jesus talks about. It is a scene that makes the Steeler fans' celebration look like polite applause at a cricket match. Emotions are raw, all barriers between people vanish. They are so overwhelmed by the moment, they can hardly stand. Hugs are infinitely tender and powerful at the same time, tears of joy flow.

All of these people had family and good friends around them every day. People whom they loved probably as much as many of the people they saved. But they would never hug them like this. Such a joyful celebration can happen only when the stakes are high, when doubt and fear press hard on all sides, where tremendous rivers of blood, sweat, and tears go into the project. Such a powerful reaction can only happen when, against all odds, the lost have been found.

That is the celebration that Jesus describes in these parables. He brings forth the revelation that God is not the all-powerful puppet master who knows all and sees all and makes the world dance to his tune.

God is the shepherd who seeks after those who are lost; God is the tunneler who is obsessed with saving those who are caught on the wrong side. It is brutally hard work, but God means to save as many people as possible. God is determined to save anyone who is beaten down by life, trapped by the consequences of bad decisions, crushed by injustice, who has fallen slave to addiction. That saving is not a sure thing, not even for God. Danger, sin, selfishness, destruction, stubbornness stand in the way. But God is relentless.

I have often wondered what people mean when they talk about God's will. So often it seems there is a preordained streak running through it. As though whatever happens, happens because God planned it down to the last detail and there was never a doubt it would take place exactly as God wanted. How is the joy that Jesus talks about even possible in such a scenario? I don't see how God's will refers to that which takes place automatically because God decreed it would. *The Tunnel* gives me a vivid, very different picture of God's will. God's will is the relentless will that never gives up; an iron will so powerful that against all odds and all obstacles, and through blood, sweat, and tears, it will accomplish God's goal of saving as many lost people as possible from the consequences of their own self-destruction.

I cannot comprehend a God who plays favorites. I can comprehend a God who cherishes the lives of all those with whom God shares relationship. And wild, ridiculous, uninhibited joy, which ranks right up at the top of the absolute greatest emotions in all of creation, comes when something happens that did not seem likely or even possible, even to God: a lost person is brought in through the tunnel, freed and given new life.

Chapter 4

I Wonder:
Does Lady Luck work for God?

At my ordination, during an otherwise exceptionally dignified occasion, one of my sons could not help but chuckle over this line in a communion hymn: "One cup of blessing which we bless," which is actually a quote from 1 Corinthians. The image struck him as bizarre. Are we *getting* a blessing here or *giving* one? How do you bless a blessing that you are receiving? Doesn't that mean we're blessing ourselves, and does that make any sense? I guess wondering about religious issues runs in the family.

I didn't have an answer for him then, but I thought of his confusion when I came across a famous passage from Genesis where God says to Abram, "I will make of you a great nation, and I will *bless* you, and make your name great, so that you will be a *blessing*. I will *bless* those who *bless* you, and in you all the families of the earth shall be *blessed*." You almost get dizzy following the bouncing blessings through that passage. What *do* we mean by that word? Are blessings, as many Christians define them, special perks and benefits that God delivers to a select few? How, then, do we deal with Scripture that says, "I will bless the Lord at all times." Are we claiming we will give special favors to God, who is fortunate to get them?

We ask God to bless our food at meal times. We want God to give special favors to a lucky cheeseburger? And how about the liturgy in the Catholic confessional: "Bless me father, for I have sinned." Give me special favors because I have sinned? Some translations substitute the word "happy" for blessed in the Beatitudes of Matthew. "Happy are those who hunger and thirst after righteousness." Well, the Bible says that God blessed the Sabbath Day. God made the Sabbath Day happy?

Look at all the ways that we use the term blessing. We are

told to bless those who persecute us. *God bless America*, say our bumper stickers. We bless people when they sneeze. We tell miserable people to count their blessings. When someone dies, we say, "Blessed be their memory." We say it's a blessing that a suffering person dies quietly in her sleep. The Bible tells us that blessed is the name of the Lord. We say that God has blessed us by giving us more stuff than other people have.

It seems we use the word as if we all know exactly what it is, when in reality it's one of the more confusing concepts in all of religion. Blessing has come to mean pretty much whatever you want it to mean. It's a catch all utility word for something good. It's the biblical version of duct tape. There's hardly anything you can't use it for. Which is why I have had so much trouble understanding blessings. A word that can mean so many things ends up meaning nothing at all. Or worse, we create our own meaning for it. Just what is a blessing?

The standard definition of blessing today is the one used back in the early days of the Old Testament. That is the view of blessings as tangible things—such as fame, fortune, influence, large flocks—given as special favors to select people. The implication is that God favors these lucky ones over other people who don't have fame, fortune, influence, and large flocks. This is consistent with Old Testament stories in which parents give a special blessing to one of their children, generally the oldest male. This lucky child gets more than the others. He gets special favors. So are blessings, in fact, special favors given to the fortunate few? I have done a lot of wondering about that. It just sounds so ... pagan!

In early pagan cultures, there was no such thing as luck, or fortune, or chance. Whatever you got, you got because the gods decided to give it to you. The gods could either bless you or curse you. Power and riches came to those who were favored or blessed by the gods. The trick to getting ahead in life was to figure out how to get on the gods' good side so that they would give you what you wanted.

How has Christianity changed our view of divine manipulation of fortune? From where I'm sitting, not much. People still tend to view God as the great Santa Claus in the sky. Checking if you've been naughty or nice. Giving blessings in the form of success and material rewards to those who deserve it. Giving curses in the form of bad luck to those who don't pass muster. That's what the Prosperity Gospel that is so popular now preaches. That isn't the God of the Bible. That isn't Christianity; it's ancient paganism.

As evidence of how deeply Christians are steeped in pagan ways, I submit a news report some years ago about a woman canoeing in a remote area of Northern Wisconsin. As she passed under a tree overhanging the river, a large branch broke off, struck the woman on the head, and killed her. The news article quoted the county sheriff as saying, "Something like that, it's just one of those acts of God."

An act of God? Think about it. God has decided that this woman must die. Now there are dozens of the usual ways God could kill her: heart attack, car accident, disease. But no, God is a little bored today and decides to try something a little more fun and challenging. God's going to calculate the exact speed of the river current, the positioning of the canoe, and making allowances for the wind, knock a branch loose at exactly the right instant to hit her on the head. Booya! Nailed it!

That isn't the God of the Bible. That isn't Christianity. We twist Christianity into paganism when we blame God for every unlucky occurrence, and thank God for all the blessings that God controls from God's great distribution center. We thank God for blessings of providing us with a good job, a comfortable house, for the money to buy all kinds of toys and conveniences. I know of a woman who thanked God for finding her a parking space in a busy mall. Yes, God's been good to us. God has blessed us and given us so much.

It takes the witness of the poor, who understand the beatitudes better than we do, to puncture that pagan bubble. If you say that God has blessed you with wealth, you are saying God doesn't care about the billions of people living in crushing poverty, whom God has chosen not to bless.

If you say that God has blessed you with abundant food, you are saying that God considers you so much more deserving than the thousands of children whose bodies are wasting as they cry themselves to sleep from hunger.

If you thank God for keeping you safe and healthy in your home, you are saying that God likes you better than all those innocent people killed by tsunamis, earthquakes, hurricanes, and terrorist attacks. You can view financial and career success as blessings from God only if you are willing to concede that God has no problem also rewarding those who gain *their* wealth and success by cheating, cutting corners, and exploiting people.

God *has* given the world ample material gifts. We have more than enough resources to satisfy every person on earth. When we thank God for material blessings, as we certainly ought to do, we thank God for providing those gifts to the world.

But the poor remind us that God does not bless people by manipulating the distribution system so that a favored few get more than others. There's a difference between being blessed and having more than other people. There's a difference between being blessed and being lucky. In our weekly confession, we are called to repent of our glib assumption that we are entitled to our great fortune in life. That the reason we have more than others in the world is because God has chosen to give us more.

So is the Bible, which seems to use so many diverse definitions of blessing, going to be of any help in sorting out the difference between blessings and luck? I think it could be. What if one of the themes of the Bible is the story of how our understanding of blessing has changed over time, as God gradually got people to understand who God is. Our current bewilderment may result from our accepting all the definitions over time instead of recognizing how the Bible chronicles the changes in how we understand blessing and luck.

Abraham was born into the pagan world view. In his world, when God promised to bless him, that meant he had it made. He was on God's good side and that meant he was going to get special favors: fame and riches. All he had to do was follow God's rules, and the gravy train was open for business. Again, there was no such thing as luck or good fortune. The rules were simple. Do good; you'll be rich and well fed. Do bad, and you'll be hungry and homeless.

Abraham got it wrong, like he got a lot of things wrong. The Old Testament writers started to figure this out fairly early. People could not help but notice that virtue and riches did not always go together. The book of Job was a daring attempt to face the evidence that being good does not guarantee power and riches or good health or smooth sailing. People don't always get what they deserve.

Ecclesiastes goes so far as to say: "Again I saw that under the sun the race is not to the swift, nor battle to the strong, nor bread to the wise, nor riches to the intelligent, nor favor to men of skill; but time and chance happen to them all." Hey, there *is* such a thing as luck, says the wise old preacher of Ecclesiastes, and it doesn't necessarily have anything to do with God.

When we hit the Psalms, we see more effects of this transition in attitude. There are dozens of references to blessings, and almost none of them have to do with riches and good fortune:

Blessed are those whose strength is in God.

Blessed is the one whom God corrects, blessed is he who has regard for the poor.

Blessed is he who comes in the name of the Lord.

The Psalms say who is blessed but don't say a lot about what it means to be blessed, which doesn't help those of us who are wondering about what blessings mean. It's not until we come to the beatitudes of the gospels that we finally get a real handle on what blessing is all about. It's a bit of a shock at first. When Jesus talks about blessing, riches, fortune, and power are not even in the picture.

Blessed are the poor in spirit. Humility has no connection to riches and fortune.

Blessed are those who mourn. You mourn over loss, over misfortune. In other words, Jesus is saying blessed are those who are *not* favored—who have bad luck.

Blessed are the meek, the merciful, the pure in heart, the peacemakers, the persecuted. If there's anyone who isn't enjoying the gravy train, it is the persecuted. Their lives are full of misfortune, and yet they are blessed. In Jesus' view the unlucky, the powerless, the poor, the gentle people who get walked all over and taken advantage of, are blessed. Could he make it any clearer that being blessed has nothing to do with wealth, or good fortune, or even adequate food and housing?

By what reasoning, then, does God call these people blessed? Because of what will happen to them? That's part of it. In these passages, some of the blessings have to do with the future. God still doles out good fortune; it's just that for some, it's being deferred into the next life. You may not feel lucky right now, but your luck will turn. You shall see God, you shall inherit the earth, you shall find reward in heaven.

But there's a problem with that, expressed by the poet Alexander Pope: "Hope springs eternal in the human breast. Man never is but always to be blessed." That's the conclusion that comes from viewing Christianity as only the promise of a change in our luck in the afterlife, in viewing Christianity as a drug that numbs us to the hardships of this life by promising a better future.

Such thinking ignores a big chunk of what the beatitudes say about blessings. "Blessed are the poor in spirit for theirs is the kingdom of heaven." It doesn't say theirs will be the kingdom of heaven. Theirs *is* the kingdom of heaven. Now.

This blessing is not something that will eventually come to the poor in spirit, those who mourn, those who are persecuted, those who suffer for going against the grain of society in seeking peace and justice. Those people are blessed now.

As I ponder this, I wonder if the early Old Testament writers were on the right track after all. A blessing *is* God's special favor, but maybe it doesn't come in the form that we expect. The special favor is that God claims us as God's own children. God blesses us by acting in love toward us as a parent to a child. When we ask God to bless us or anyone or anything, we are simply asking God to be present as a parent is to a child.

This still leaves a problem that makes me squirm. No responsible parent plays favorites among his or her children. So why is God's presence not evenly distributed among all people? Why are blessings in the beatitudes concentrated on the poor in spirit, the mourning, the persecuted, the people who are struggling to live good lives? It sounds at first like a difficult question. But then I ask myself, when am I most intensely giving to my children? Not when luck is smiling on them, when everything is going their way, when they're rolling in wealth. My children have needed their parents most when they felt beaten by life, when they were scared, when they were cut from a sports team, when they were betrayed by friends, when they were hurt in a car accident or sledding mishap, when they were discouraged or devastated, when something for which they poured out their heart and soul was taken from them.

Similarly, I'm convinced that God blesses us at all times, in the highs and the lows of this world. But God blesses you most—God is most present as a parent to you—when you have been slammed by life, when you are in the deepest throes of mourning, when you are being hounded by enemies, when life hurts so bad you can hardly stand it, when your luck is the absolute worst it can be.

Being humble, meek, and merciful, and working for peace don't get you very far in this world, but it brings God's blessing. Being pure in heart and hungering and thirsting after righteousness is not the way to amass a fortune, but it is a way to know God's loving presence up close and personal, and to know that God means it when God promises to wipe away every tear, and that a day will come when there is no more hunger, no more thirst.

The benediction is a blessing we give at the end of the worship service, and we give it to the lucky and the unlucky. At seminary, I was taught never to say, "*May* the Lord bless and keep you," when pronouncing the benediction. We are not wishing for God's blessing; we are not asking for God's blessing. In saying those words, says God, "You shall put my name on the people, and I *will* bless them. I will be with them as a parent." In that blessing, we upon whom time, chance, and fortune have worked their ways, are claimed as God's children. When I think of it that way, I guess I do feel lucky.

Chapter 5

I Wonder:
Does God Have Ego Issues?

There is a deep strain of Christian thought that says the purpose of life is to glorify God. The way to accomplish this glorification is to praise God. My question is why? I don't question whether God deserves praise; I'm just wondering how much does God want it?

Praise is a big thing in modern worship, especially in contemporary worship. The standard format for such services is to start with two or three praise songs. There are services where praise songs take up the first 20 minutes to a half hour. Most contemporary Christian music written today has to do with praise. Choirs are often referred to as Praise Teams, instrumentalists as the Praise Band.

Of course, this emphasis on praise is not entirely new. It has a long tradition, as these words from the old standby hymn *Amazing Grace* indicate: "When we've been there 10,000 years, bright shining as the sun, we've no less days to sing God's praise, then when we've first begun." It's not hard to see where this tradition of praise originated. It comes mostly from Psalms. Within a span of three verses in Psalm 67, we are told no fewer than four times to "let the peoples praise God."

Why does so much of our relationship with God consist of praise? The question occurred to me after I was given a sendoff from my internship congregation in Spooner, WI. They asked me to stand in the pulpit while the congregation sang to me ten verses of a song they had written called "Amazing Nate," to the tune of *Amazing Grace*. Now this was a wonderful congregation. I know they meant well, and I realize it was a tremendous honor. But as I was shrinking in discomfort, listening to this tribute go on for what seemed an excruciating eternity, the notion hit me:

If God is half as uncomfortable with our singing praises to God as I am right now listening to this, I'm going to have to seriously rethink this whole praise business.

So I wonder, not out of a desire to be cute or clever or annoying, what is the point of all this praise? And it's no good saying that's just the way God is and the ways of God surpass all understanding. The Bible tells us a great deal about God and it stands to reason that God does not desire things that are inconsistent with who God is.

Let's go at it this way: What are some possible reasons why anyone would want to be praised? How about appeasement? Since time immemorial, mortals have been afraid of gods. In many societies, religion has been based on the idea that our behavior angers the gods and we need to do something to calm that anger.

Many Christians believe that God is a demanding sort, with a cruel sense of justice and a terrible temper, the kind of being who could damn people to an eternity of fiery torture for not believing the right things. You do not want to get this kind of God mad. So, praise can serve as kind of a buffer to keep God at bay. Like a slave bowing and scraping before a powerful master, hoping not to offend so that he can escape punishment. Is that what our praise accomplishes? Well, there is no doubt that God can get angry, and that we do all kinds of things that God does not like. But is praise going to have any effect on that situation? As if we are God's psychiatrists, able to control God's anger by administering large doses of praise.

No, I cannot believe that praise is an anger management technique. We do not sing praises to appease an angry God. How about the flip side of appeasement? Flattery. There is a common view, noted in the previous chapter, that God is standing just off to the side of our lives, dangling the keys to our fate in his hand. If God likes you, you'll be rewarded and your life will be easy. If God doesn't like you, things are not going to go well. If that is the way things are then it pays to get on God's good side. What better way to do it than praise? Everyone responds well to praise, don't they? Keep telling God how great God is, God likes that, so God responds by rewarding you.

Do you see a problem with this image of God? Again, it assumes we can manage God. It assumes that God is either too vain or too stupid to recognize a manipulation so transparent that most of us would spot it in a second. No, I cannot believe praise is a way of buttering up the boss. We do not sing praises to flatter God.

Do we praise God because God demands or requires it? That seems a little more reasonable and it is another common Christian view. At least this view recognizes that God is in control. Praise is something that God likes and desires and it is our duty as creatures made by God to provide it to our Creator. So we come to church because it is our duty or obligation and we praise God because it's required of us.

But again, I have to wonder about this image of God as someone who demands praise. If you praise me only because I demand it, how sincere is that praise? Does it mean anything? No, God did not create people to be flunkies and toadies. We do not sing praises because God demands it.

Then perhaps praise is simply recognition for a job well done. I think here we are starting to get closer to the mark. God *is* a great and wonderful being who has done marvelous things. We are not lying or even exaggerating when we praise God. When we praise God, we are simply giving credit where credit is due.

There is just one problem with this view of praise. Remember, the question we are asking is why would God want to be praised. While recognition for our accomplishments is something we all appreciate, is that what motivates God? Is God so insecure that God needs assurance of success to maintain self-esteem?

Some of the most revered people in the world are those who give or do things anonymously. They purposely avoid publicity and shun recognition for their good works. We admire that kind of selflessness. Many of these people are not religious at all. Doesn't it seem strange for a Christian to argue that such folks are far more selfless and admirable than God, especially when we learned from Jesus Christ that selflessness is perhaps the prime characteristic of God?

We're not getting very far in our wondering, are we? So far, we have not come up with a single good reason why God would want or need our praise. In fact, as we read the Bible, particularly the Old Testament which deals most with praise, we find the Israelites were not in agreement as to why or whether God wanted to be praised. Some verses suggest that the Israelites thought God could be appeased by praise, some suggest that God expects or demands praise. Other verses, particularly in Amos, emphatically declare that God has no particular interest in being praised. So just what is the place of praise in our worship?

My current view of what praise of God is all about comes from an incident that happened many years ago. My daughter was about four years old when she and my wife were visiting friends several blocks down the street. Mikhaila was playing in the yard with a friend who was her age, while the adults visited in the house. Rather abruptly, she decided it was time to go home. Being an independent little girl, she did not tell anyone she was going. She just started walking.

Unfortunately, she missed the turn that would have taken her home. Still convinced she was on the right track, she kept walking and walking. I don't know if this story plays as well in a small town, but in a city, a four-year-old getting lost walking away from her neighborhood is a scary thing.

Our mail carrier happened to notice her walking. He was someone who paid close attention to his surroundings, and he knew his customers. He knew where this little girl lived and saw that she was walking, alone, in the wrong direction. He crossed the street to talk to her and got her pointed in the right direction.

That was not all he did. He watched to make sure she made the one turn that he directed her to make. Then he went up to a house and asked to use their phone. (This was in the days before cell phones.) He looked up our number and called the house, where I was working in my office. He told me what had happened so that I could keep an eye out for her to make sure she got home. She made it just fine, and about 45 minutes later, when delivering mail to our house, the carrier rang the doorbell. Just making sure that she got home safely.

Forgive me if I don't join in when people criticize the U.S. Postal Service. For the rest of the day, I had a difficult time working. I kept thinking about what that mail carrier had done, so far beyond the expected. I was so overwhelmed by his actions that I could not concentrate on anything else until I wrote a letter to his superior, telling what had happened that day. That letter was overflowing with praise.

I did not write that letter because it was expected or required. I did not write it to flatter or to appease. Although it gave credit where credit was due, that was not my primary motivation for writing it. I sent that letter of praise to the mail carrier for one simple reason: I couldn't help it. I needed to tell someone how fantastic that mailman was, and until I could, I really didn't have anything else to say. The mail carrier did not do what he did in hopes of getting a letter like that. Praise was not even on his radar. In his actions that day, he was simply being who he was. And yet, I think my letter made his day.

So it is with our praise. God does not do what God does in hopes or expectation of praise. When God creates a world full of wonder and blessings to share with us, God is simply being who God is. When we sing praises to God, we are not appeasing a bully. We are not flattering someone with ego issues, or someone who gets a kick out of ordering pathetic little underlings to tell God how good he is. We are not simply giving credit where credit is due. God doesn't need our praise. We praise God not because God needs to hear it, but because we need to give it.

True praise happens when we are so overwhelmed by the scope and the majesty of what God has done for us that we cannot go on with our lives until we say something.

We gather together in church to praise, not out of obligation or duty, but because we simply cannot get through the week without expressing a response to that unfathomable love. When that happens, I think we make God's day.

Chapter 6

I Wonder:
Why Is the God of the Old Testament So Violent?

When I talk to people who reject the Christian message, one of the greatest obstacles to belief they cite is the book of Joshua. Specifically, they recoil at Bible passages which depict God as an advocate of genocide. This claim that God is a vengeful, bloodthirsty tyrant who orders the mass murders of entire populations and even punishes those who show mercy is too much for many people to swallow.

Frankly, it should be. It is for me, and I find it at least somewhat encouraging that the spark of curiosity and wonder still retains the power to break through at least the most egregious of religious authorities' questionable doctrines.

The overall theme of the Bible is that God is love. The view that God mercilessly demands blood and suffering is squarely at odds with that. So does the book of Joshua prove the Bible to be a worthless mass of contradictions, or is there somehow room in the divine nature to be both merciful and merciless? Like many people, I have wondered about this question for a long time. Here is where my wondering has taken me:

When we talk about faith journeys, we almost always focus on experiences in faith that have shaped our individual lives. But would it not be just as valuable to reflect on the faith journey of the Christian community? Before we begin, let us postulate that the Bible is not an instruction manual or a collection of legal ordinances dictated by God. It is the book of faith, which Christians believe to have been inspired by God and designed to create faith. It is a library of writings from many different genres. Together these writings tell the story of how the faith that emerged in the early chapters of the Bible grew into something entirely different and infinitely more life-changing by the time we hit Galatians.

Let's take a moment to review the entire Bible, and in so doing, try to keep up with the Holy Spirit as it crashes through barrier after barrier, and finally unleashes the love of God into all creation.

The Bible begins with two creation stories. The first (Genesis 1) proclaims God as the creator of the world in which we live. The second (Genesis 2) proclaims God as the one who brought human life into being. Why did God create all this? The Bible says it is because God is a loving being, who wants to share love with others, who created humans for the purpose of developing a relationship with them.

A loving relationship can happen only when both parties have freedom to choose the relationship or decline it, and so God gave humans that freedom. With the freedom to choose love comes the freedom not to choose love. The early stories of Genesis declare that God's plan flew off the tracks because humans chose not to love. They chose not to return the love God gave them, much less reflect it to others.

The earth, meant to be a garden of prosperity and harmony, fell into turmoil and ruin. Humans seemed utterly unable to do anything about it. As things bottomed out, God was faced with a choice: Scrub the place clean and start over, or do something to fix it. This was not going to be an easy fix. Under human management, creation had deteriorated badly. The list of repairs God had to make was daunting. Here's what God had to start with on the reclamation project:

1. People don't know the first thing about God. Their faith consists mainly of superstition. They believe their lives are controlled by multiple gods, who are arbitrary, capricious, and morally corrupt. If you bribe and flatter them, they will make you rich and successful. If you screw up, they will curse you.

2. People have somehow come to believe that one of the things the gods enjoy is the smell of burning blood, including the blood of children. As a result, they practice child sacrifice.

3. People are brutal. They are constantly at war, and subscribe to the principle of kill others before they kill you. They will avenge any wrong done to them, swiftly and without mercy. Genocide is acceptable because it eliminates potentially deadly enemies.

4. People are suspicious of strangers and anyone who is not like them.

5. People believe themselves and their clan to be superior to others and so they feel entitled to enslave whomever they wish. They view slaves as their personal property — they can beat them and even kill them if they wish.

6. They believe widows and orphans are a burden to society and they feel no obligation to waste precious resources helping them.

7. They believe those with disabilities are being punished either for their sins or the sins of their parents. They are inferior people who do not have the same rights as the rest of society.

8. They believe that women have no rights. Men are the only ones allowed to hold power, make decisions, own property. Men practice polygamy and are quite tolerant of rape.

9. They are grossly ignorant about the natural world that God created.

That's what God has to start with. How can God possibly redeem people like this and restore creation to peace and prosperity? The rational thing seems to be to destroy it all and start fresh. But God's nature is love. Because God loves creation, including humans, God does not want to destroy it. So God rolls up the sleeves and goes to work on the monumental project of rehabilitating humankind, beginning with Abraham.

God says to Abraham, "Your understanding of me is wrong. I don't want you as my toy, my plaything to amuse me; I want a relationship with you. I need you to trust me. If you do that, then we can begin to remake the world. Then we can begin to knock down the barriers that stand in the way of peace and prosperity."

Abraham says, "Okay. I don't know you at all. I don't understand you at all, but I will trust you." Because of that, things can get rolling.

The first barrier to go is child sacrifice. Genesis 22 tells the story of when Abraham nearly killed his son Isaac as a sacrifice to God. In that story Abraham comes to understand that is not what God requires. That's not who God is.

This barrier is relatively easy to knock down because the idea of child sacrifice is so repulsive. Once you get past the Abraham-Isaac incident, there is no more talk of child sacrifice in the Bible.

Other barriers are more difficult to dismantle, yet we see the spirit of God working in people. You think widows and orphans are a burden and should be left to fend for themselves? Not in my world, says God.

What about strangers? The world is never going to be as God desires if you are scared of people you don't know and decide to blow them away. Goaded by God's repeated command to tend to the stranger, the widow, and the orphan, the Israelites change. They incorporate protections for these people in their laws. By the time of the prophets, this sort of compassion, which was once unknown, is understood to be the bedrock of who God's people are.

How about this superstition that the world is full of multiple gods who control every aspect of life? That's tougher to eradicate.

The spirit of God works on this misconception in the words of Deuteronomy 6:4, *Hear O Israel, the Lord our God, the Lord is one.* Eventually, that verse becomes a cornerstone of faith. But the old superstitions keep cropping up. In Psalm 135, for example, we hear "I know that the Lord is great, our Lord is above all gods." Who are these other gods you're talking about? Remember, the Lord our God, the Lord is one.

How about the view that you have to bribe and flatter God to be successful? Again, the spirit has tough sledding on that. As we have seen, in Abraham's mind, when God promised to bless him, that meant he had it made. All he had to do was dance to God's tune, and he had it made. Do good; you'll be rich and well fed. Do bad, and God will see that you are hungry and homeless. Gradually, we see that attitude begin to change as the Spirit works through Job, through Ecclesiastes, and the Psalms to a new understanding of blessing.

How about holy war; the bloodthirsty attitudes toward enemies? At first, the Israelites incorporated their taste for violence into their view of God. God is on our side, they believe. God wants evil-doers wiped off the face of the earth. In their books of Joshua and Judges, they understood God as endorsing their warfare, and even genocide. But through the work of the Spirit, by the end of the Old Testament, genocide has faded from the picture; violence becomes less prevalent. What about ignorance of God's world? Through the words of Proverbs, the spirit of God leads people to pursue knowledge, wisdom and truth.

By the end of the Old Testament, here's the progress report on God's plan to salvage creation:

Successes:
Child sacrifice—gone
Genocide—gone
Polygamy—gone
Multiple Gods—gone
Partial Successes:
Superstition—some people are beginning to understand God's grace

Suspicion of strangers — making progress
Disdain for the powerless in society (widows and orphans) —
making progress
Ignorance of God and God's creation — making progress.
Failures:
Slavery — still prevalent and officially approved
Those with disabilities — still considered inferior or evil
People who are different — still feared
Women — still have no rights or status.

Some prevailing ideas and attitudes were so entrenched that the spirit of God could not change people. Then God sent Jesus to earth to show people what God was all about.

Jesus taught that God cannot be bribed or flattered into granting riches and power. In fact, God is most present with those who have the least.

Jesus taught that violence is not the answer. He urged people to turn the other cheek, love their enemies and pray for them.

At a time when society ridiculed lepers, epileptics, the blind, and others with health issues and disabilities, Jesus welcomed them, respected them, and healed them. Disdain for people who were different was so entrenched that even Jesus had to stretch out of his comfort zone to deal with this. When he met a Canaanite woman who asked for healing, he initially declined to help. After all, he had come for the Jews. But by the end of that encounter, he broke through that barrier and from then on taught that we are to welcome disciples of all nations.

Jesus taught that Christians are to be servants of others, just as Christ served us. He repeatedly emphasized that we are put on this earth to love as God loved us. He then showed exactly what this love looks like when he suffered and died for the sake of all humankind. What Jesus taught and did had earth-shattering implications for many issues, including slavery and sexism. But these ideas were so entrenched that people did not understand the implications.

So the Spirit worked through the mind of the Apostle Paul, who put it all together in a simple, startling statement in his letter to the Galatians: *There is no longer Jew or Greek, there is no longer slave or free, there is no longer male and female; for all of you are one in Christ Jesus.* That sentence, which would have astounded anyone living in that time, was the key to wiping out all the remaining barriers that stood in the way of God's purpose for creation.

Let's look back at what God's incredibly difficult, painstaking, agonizing effort to redeem creation had achieved. One by one, it had shattered seemingly insurmountable barriers to peace and prosperity that were destroying God's creation.

The world in which Paul lived was a different place from the mess that God had started with. The world had changed; it was different not because God changed, but God relentlessly shaped a people made in God's image, a people filled with love.

The story is not over. The effort at redemption is far from finished. The barriers are not gone. Even Paul had trouble catching up with the message that he proclaimed. Like Thomas Jefferson, who preached eloquently on the equality of man, yet held dozens of slaves, Paul struggled to live up to what he preached in Galatians. He did not quite get all the implications of his message regarding slaves, or women, or those who were different. That's what sin is all about. Christians have been struggling to catch up with the trail-blazing work of the Holy Spirit ever since.

Christians were defending slavery until the mid-nineteenth century. We didn't begin to recognize the dignity of those with disabilities until the twentieth century.

We didn't begin to address barriers to women until that same late date, and many Christians continue to support those barriers to this day. Christians are still leading the charge in endorsing the scientific ignorance. There are Christians who continue to promote violence, hostility to strangers, and contempt for the poor and for those who are different.

When people say that mainline Christianity is falling away from our sacred tradition, what do they mean? It appears to me that they want us to return to a society that was so messed up that God came this close to destroying the whole thing.

I do not understand Christians who hold out the fallen, broken material God had to work with in Genesis as the ideal of who we ought to be and how we ought to act. I hope and pray we *are* getting away from the roots of our Christian tradition, because that tradition began in a cruel, polygamous, child-sacrificing, superstitious, racist, genocidal, slave-owning, sexist, xenophobic, scientifically ignorant society.

Praise God that the life of Jesus Christ and the work of the Holy Spirit is leading us out of that place. The faster and further the Holy Spirit can usher us out of that place and into the love of Jesus Christ, the better. Because when we truly live in a place where there is neither Jew or Greek, slave or free, male or female, and all of us are truly one, then creation will finally start to look the way God intended it.

Part II

Questions about Jesus

Chapter 7

I Wonder:
Other than some isolated field hands, nobody reported a thing on that first Christmas. Why?

As we were singing Christmas carols one year, it suddenly hit me that a medley of those songs can give one emotional whiplash. Have you ever noticed how our Christmas carols seem to fall into polar opposite camps? Take, for example, the following crossfire of dueling Christmas carols:

Oh, Come all ye faithful, Joyful and triumphant! Come ye, O come ye to Bethlehem!

O Little town of Bethlehem, how still we see thee lie.

Above the deep and dreamless sleep ...

Sing choirs of angels, sing in exultation; sing all ye citizens of heaven above!

How silently, how silently, the wondrous gift is given.

Joyful all you nations rise, join the triumph of the skies!

The world in solemn stillness lay ...

While fields and floods, rocks hills and plains repeat the sounding joy!

Silent night, holy night, all is calm ...

And heaven and nature sing, And heaven and nature sing.

Sleep in heavenly peace, Sleep in heavenly peace.

As with our Thanksgiving celebration, it makes you wonder, just how are we supposed to celebrate the season of Christmas? With back-pounding, ear-splitting explosions of joy and celebration over the arrival of the Savior of the world? Or with quiet, reverent, almost whispering lullabies as we try to comprehend the awesome mystery of the event.

As I read through Luke's Christmas story, it occurred to me that Luke does not make that choice clear. At first glance, it seems that what we are hearing about is a blow-out celebration with the volume cranked as high as it can go. An angel appears in the shepherds' fields, in a blaze of glory so blinding that he scares the poor guys half to death. After announcing the birth of the Savior, suddenly there was with the angel a multitude of the heavenly host—we're talking hundreds, maybe thousands of angels—praising God and saying, "Glory to God in the highest!"

It appears that the whole world is rockin', the universe breaks out in fireworks, and a massed host of heavenly beings thunder out a joyful noise beyond imagination, a deafening crescendo of song unlike anything the world has ever seen. Except that when we look at this more closely, that does not seem to be what is happening at all. As you study the story, you notice that this universal exclamation of joy is not so universal. The entire celebration takes place only above a field in an isolated, rural location. It is neither thunderous nor deafening. The only ones in the cosmos who hear the rejoicing in the cosmos are a few shepherds in a field. No one else in the whole world heard anything special that night. It appears likely that every person in the next village slept through the whole thing. There is no evidence that those looking up at the stars in the next county that night noticed anything out of the ordinary.

In other words, other than a small group of minimum-wage field hands out in a remote area, nobody saw or heard a thing on that Christmas evening. In later years, people in the town of Nazareth where Jesus grew up did not seem to know anything about what happened that evening. If they had heard even a hint about this angel chorus at his birth, they would have known he was something special as he grew up. But when he began his ministry of healing, they seemed surprised. Stunned, even. "Who is this guy to think he is anything special?" they asked.

News of an astounding event like the angel chorus would have traveled fast, you would think, and yet according to Matthew, the king of the land, Herod, who had informants in every area of the country, never heard anything about it until many months later, when a few astrologers from a faraway region of the world wandered into the country, asking about an arrangement of stars they had seen in the sky.

How could so spectacular an event be so spectacularly missed? How did something that caused an explosion of celebration in heaven and a massive chorus of angels singing in the middle of the night slip under the radar? In fact, the silence and stillness, and calm and peaceful sleep of the other Christmas carols seem to be a more accurate description of what was going on in that little stable, and much of the world that night.

That being the case, what do we make of the part of the story that talks about huge heavenly choirs breaking into the night sky over the shepherds' field in a rousing celebration? What do we make of the fields and floods, rocks, hills and plains, all repeating the sounding joy! Of heaven and nature and singing?

The whole thing seems baffling. How come in this Gospel story, no one else but shepherds even caught a glimpse or heard a peep from the explosion of joy at this crucial moment in the history of the universe? It's a fascinating dynamic, and wondering about that opened my eyes to a new possibility as to what the Christmas story is all about.

God created the world as an expression of love. As a way to share love and joy and peace with others. But humans kept messing it up. Selfishness and greed kept poisoning the well, leading to all kinds of troubles: wars, poverty, hatred, misery. That's not what God had in mind at all.

As we have discussed earlier, throughout the Old Testament, God attempted to get people to adopt a better way of life, but humans were having none of it. Yes, some people made attempts at living in harmony with God in the way that would lead to prosperity and peace, but in the end, selfishness always seemed to win out and make a mess of things. God realized that humans would never bring about peace on earth; they had to be brought into it. They had to be shown what love is. They had to experience love in a demonstration so real and powerful and stunning that it would break through the cynicism and complacency and self-centeredness that characterizes the human race. The situation called for an event that would shine the light of truth on the world and blaze forth forever more as a beacon of that truth, so that even the short-sighted, short-memoried, backsliding inhabitants of creation would have a constant, meaningful reminder of who God is, and how peace on earth is possible.

Jesus entered the world in a stable, not a palace, because a palace would not have shown us anything worthwhile about God. Humans love wealth and privilege too much as it is. If Jesus were to come to earth enjoying wealth and privilege and power, that would only reinforce the idea that these things are what it's all about. That would demonstrate that the only difference between us and God is that God is lucky enough to be able to get whatever God wants. That God is all about getting and not giving.

The Christmas story says that Jesus entered the world as a helpless baby, not as a divine emperor because a divine emperor is all about power. Babies have no power. God is not about wielding power, but about giving.

Jesus entered the world as part of an insignificant peasant family, not as a royal prince because nobility of birth is all about putting some people above others, and that would not have shown us anything about God. God is about giving.

Jesus entered the world in the dirt and dust without so much as a single new outfit or toy or even a pillow, rather than in a plush palace because God isn't about acquiring material things. God is about giving. Jesus entered the world unnoticed except for a few shepherds because God isn't about grabbing attention. God is about giving.

When God chose to enter into our world, God could have come as anyone or anything God wanted, but chose to come as an utterly helpless, dirt-poor nobody. Because God is not about getting, but about giving. That was the message of Christmas.

I have read several fascinating books recently about Ulysses Grant, the Civil War general and the 18th president of the United States. Grant's most dominant characteristic was that he was so ordinary. He had absolutely no presence or charisma. Time and again Grant would enter a room crowded with people who were excited to see the hero of the Western battlefronts, and nobody saw him. He would stand there for 30 minutes and no one recognized him. He would check into a hotel where the staff were primed to go all out for this great celebrity, only to be treated rather shabbily by the staff who never imagined that this ordinary drudge in front of them was the hero of the nation.

That penchant for avoiding attention not only did not bother Grant, it was what made him a success. He understood, as no other leader in the U.S. army did, that being a general was not about the praise, the pomp, the attention, the high roller treatment that came with the position. To him, being a general was about only one thing: what he could give to his army and to his country. By focusing solely on how he could best serve, he succeeded where all other generals of the Army of the Potomac failed.

Now I am certainly not equating Grant with Jesus. Lord knows the man had his own peculiar faults and weaknesses. But it is no stretch to say that Grant saw the gift that God gave the world at Christmas. The gift of giving. The gift of knowing that what makes life worth living is not seeing what you can get from others, but what you can give.

There is no way that God could have taught that lesson by coming in glory to the halls of a palace, from underneath a satin robe and sable furs, while ordering servants about to satisfy his every whim, while commanding an invincible army. Jesus couldn't have thundering 6000-cannon salutes, heavenly fireworks, booming voices from heaven echoing throughout the world, a thousand miracles, spectacular signs. God had to come into the room unnoticed, the arrival unrecognized.

And so, silently, how silently the wondrous gift is given.

The story of Christmas is that God taught the lesson of love by giving away every advantage. By becoming a baby utterly reliant on others, a creature who did not have a lick of sense or intelligence, by signing away all rights to a life of luxury and privilege.

Therein lies an explanation for the mystery of the dueling Christmas carols. God came as someone *deserving* of praise and honor, but who chose to come silently and unrecognized.

While all of the heavens were absolutely blown away by this stunning act of love, they were caught in a paradox. They would spoil everything if they gave Jesus all the accolades that God deserved but was purposely avoiding. But the cosmos, heaven and nature, could not contain the joy that this stunning act of love brought—they had to tell somebody. This arrival of God into the world to be with us was the most miraculous, most intense outpouring of love the world has ever known.

This changed everything. A world that was going nowhere fast, now had a future. How could they not celebrate? Yet they would wreck everything if they ushered Jesus into the world with that fanfare.

The solution? The heavens could express the amazement and joy of the cosmos by sharing it with a small and unlikely group of people. By letting loose a thunderous display of sheer, irrepressible joy to people so insignificant that few others would take them seriously when they shared what they experienced. They unloaded this celebration on people who would have no effect whatsoever on Jesus' life, who could not give anything but thanks and a smile and a look of sheer amazement at this gift of life.

The first Christmas showed us clearly what God's nature is. That nature does not change. Just like in the nativity scene, God comes to each of us. Not with a swagger and one eye in the mirror. Not with fanfare announcing the royal presence. Not with mighty deeds and ridiculous feats that defy nature. Not by exercising power that crushes all foes.

God comes to us today as God did on Christmas, in love that gives and gives and gives. God comes in love that quietly guides us away from selfish destruction and shows us the way to peace and happiness. God's voice is not loud; we have to listen to hear it, as the word passes from person to person, place to place, generation to generation.

So we celebrate what happened on Christmas with those two types of carols. We remember how God came to us, in stealth, in silence, giving it all up for us. We sing *Silent Night*. And we celebrate with the universe and the angel choirs the event that rescued the world from a path of certain destruction. An event of such magnitude that we can hardly contain our joy. We sing *Joy to the World. How silently, how silently, the wondrous gift is given. Joyful all you nations rise, join the triumph of the skies. And heaven and nature sing.*

Chapter 8

I Wonder:
Did Jesus Do Magic?

As we traveled along an empty highway through open farmland north of Cadott, Wisconsin, we came across an electronic sign warning of possible traffic jams ahead. Traffic jams! Here, in the middle of nowhere? For most of the year such a sign would be ridiculous. It is there, however, because for one weekend out of the year, this area is the site of a gigantic rock festival.

As I read the story of the feeding of the five thousand, I cannot help but be reminded of that concert site. I imagine gridlocked traffic and huge crowds of people streaming from near and far. All gathering in a deserted, out-of-the-way spot, in a field, far from any population center, any permanent shelter, eager to see the rock stars do their thing.

For that's what Jesus was at this point in his ministry. He was the equivalent of a rock star. He was the latest craze in the region of Galilee. Word about his act spread like wildfire. Everyone wanted to see what this local wonder could do.

Could 5000 people even hear him or see him when he spoke? It probably did not matter. Like sitting in the top row in the end zone at Lambeau Field, you're not there because the view is so great; you're there to enjoy the experience of being present for the big event. Yet at the same time, everyone dreams of getting as close to the celebrity as they can. Personal contact would be great.

This story of the feeding of the masses is the #1 miracle story of the Bible; it appears in all four Gospels. That suggests that it is absolutely central to the message of Christianity. Was the whole point of the exercise that Jesus was a powerful Dumbledore-type wizard who could perform astounding feats of magic?

No doubt many of those in Galilee thought so. They were

there for the magic show. It seems that many Christians have taken the same attitude with this story over the years. There is a conventional wisdom that the point of the feeding of the 5000 is to demonstrate that Jesus had breathtaking magical powers and is therefore worthy of praise and worship.

That has never made sense to me, though. Look what happens in a magic act, and compare that to what Jesus did in the feeding of the five thousand.

First of all, magic acts are meant to amaze, to wow people, to impress them. You want people to watch the trick and then say, "How in the world did he do that? How did she get an elephant to disappear? How was he able to restore that 100-dollar bill after he ripped it to shreds?" You want people to be baffled and amazed as they try to comprehend how the impossible just happened. That's the whole point of doing magic.

Certainly, Jesus did amaze and baffle and impress the audience that day. They were so blown away by what they saw that they gave him five-star reviews. They gushed that he was *the prophet who is to come into the world.* They were so impressed that they decided to make him king, and they were not going to take no for an answer.

We who read the story today are just as amazed and baffled and impressed. That same question that accompanies all magic acts pops into our mind: how did he do that? How did he manage to feed 5000 people with just a basketful of fish and chips?

You can read all sorts of speculation in commentaries, all sorts of wild guesses as to how Jesus was able to make that happen. Was he able to make the food somehow multiply and regenerate itself? Did new food just keep appearing? Or was it a matter of faith and sharing? Was it that some kid came forward and was willing to trust Jesus with all the food he had brought for the occasion? And others witnessed this selfless and faithful act of sharing that Jesus inspired, and so those who had brought food were in turn inspired? They brought out their food and shared it with others so that everyone was miraculously fed, even those who had brought nothing?

We don't know. The Bible doesn't give away the secret and so we are left wondering how he did it. But this much seems obvious: Jesus did not feed the 5000 as a way of impressing and wowing the people. He was not looking for that kind of attention. In fact, he was trying very hard to avoid it.

Healing mobs of people who are in need is exhausting work. Jesus was worn out and looking for a break. There is a reason why he went off into the wilderness, into the mountains, and that was to get away from people for a while—to *avoid* attention. He retreated to a place far away from the population center precisely because there was no ready source of food available. People would have to be crazy to follow him out into the middle of nowhere. He should be safe way out there in the mountains to enjoy a little R & R.

But things didn't go the way Jesus planned. It turns out, the people *were* a little bit crazy, as often happens around rock stars and other celebrities. They came out where Jesus wasn't expecting them and had made no preparations for them. Contemplating a badly needed day off in the mountains, he suddenly found himself back on stage in front of thousands of rabid and demanding fans.

Given that situation, is he going to perform some magic to dazzle them? Not likely. The last thing he wants right now is to fuel the frenzy. We know this because of the great lengths he goes in order to avoid this. When his astounding feat of feeding the five thousand provokes a standing ovation and an outcry demanding Jesus be made king, he does not just shrug and say, "Look, if nominated, I will not run; if elected I will not serve." He goes into evasive maneuvers to get these star-crazed stalkers off his trail.

As the story continues, he retreats further back up in the mountains where no one can find him. He crosses and recrosses the Sea of Galilee at odd times, sometimes with the disciples, sometimes without, to lose the crowd. This is not someone on a victory tour. In fact, the idea that Jesus would perform miracles to win praise and worship makes no sense. If God's plan were to have Jesus perform all kinds of magic that would so astonish people that they would have to believe in and follow and worship him, he could have gotten everyone to believe in him with no sweat. His life would have been so easy. As we discussed before, he could turn donkeys into dragons, toss trees in the air like they were toothpicks, cause it literally to rain cats and dogs—you name it. Everyone would be so awed that they couldn't help but bow down before him.

That was not the plan. Jesus did not come to show off his powers. He did not feed the 5000 to demonstrate how awesome he was. There had to be something else going on here. This leads us to consider a second characteristic of magic shows. What we describe as magic is always less than it appears. Magic shows are so appealing because something incredible, even impossible, appears to be happening. The key word is *appears*. Magic is really all about hype and misdirection and illusion. What appears to be happening isn't really happening.

Most of us cannot do what a magician does. Does that mean he or she possesses powers that normal human beings don't have? No, it just means that the magician knows a trick that you don't know. If he were to tell you how he did it, you would no longer be impressed with his powers. So he doesn't tell you. Because, like all magic shows, what he actually did is far less impressive than it seems.

Compare that to what happened on the mountainside near Galilee. We have a huge crowd and very little food. Too many people; too few resources. A dangerous shortage. People are going to go hungry. That's what *appears* to be the case. But whereas magic is always less than it appears in reality, in this case there was far *more* than anyone imagined. The story does not tell us how he did it; it only tells us why he did it—because he had compassion on them. When Jesus acts in compassion, scarcity is exposed as an illusion.

As I have wondered about this scene, I have become convinced that this was not a magic show on the shores of Galilee; something far more profound and meaningful and life-changing was taking place here. I have occasionally heard stories from a church or individual about how when they have found themselves in serious need, as if by magic, God provided exactly what they needed. While I do not flat-out reject such testimony, there is a crucial element of the feeding of the five thousand that is missing in them.

Jesus did not calculate the shortfall and then magically produce exactly the amount required. The disciples collected 12 basketsful of leftovers. Not only was there more available than they thought, there was more than they needed. That seems characteristic of God's grace and compassion. God is neither miserly, nor thrifty, nor even efficient. God's grace and compassion are never rationed out. They are given generously and extravagantly. We are trapped in our illusions of scarcity and our world suffers for it. Surrounded by abundance, all we see is scarcity.

When I was in college, a friend of mine designed an independent study that demonstrated to me why this is so. He was able to implant (in an era before PETA), an electrode in the hypothalamus of rats, the area of the brain known to be the center for feelings of desire and fulfillment. This electrode was hooked up to a push bar in a cage. Every time a rat touched the bar, it would get a jolt of euphoria. It took a few days for the rat to figure out the connection, but once it did, it was all over. The rat kept coming back to the bar for more. It could not focus on anything else. It did not eat, drink, or sleep. It became so obsessed with that little jolt of electricity that it could not focus on anything else, and literally starved itself to death. Surrounded by more food and water than it needed, in a nurturing environment, the rat created its own world of scarcity, in which it could not get what it needed to survive.

Now we humans are not as stupid as rats, and would never do anything so ridiculous, right? Then how do you explain the billions of dollars that we spend jolting the hypothalamus? The percentage of resources spent on entertainment, comfort, and convenience increases every year and crowds out those things that bring life—food, water, education, and spiritual concerns. We cut programs that provide these things for those in need, claiming we have no choice because we live in a world of scarcity.

There are days when all we can see is scarcity. We blame God for the fact that there is so much need and want in the world. So much hunger, disease, poverty, violence, and suffering. We feel there's nothing we can do; we don't have the resources to cope with it. All we have is five loaves of bread and two small fish, and what is that among so many?

But then just as I'm wondering why there is so much scarcity in our world, I am treated to a modern-day version of the feeding of the five thousand. I refer to the Wild Boars soccer team in Thailand who found themselves trapped in a cave by swiftly rising monsoon waters, leaving them with virtually no resources. They were trapped more than a mile underground in an area so remote it had not been mapped in 70 years, with no food, light, warmth, sanitary conditions, cell phone or GPS service: cut off by miles of underground currents raging through narrow, winding passageways that would task the strongest and most experienced divers in the world. It seemed there were not enough resources in the world to find them, much less rescue them.

But when compassion is unleashed, it turns out what appears to be scarcity is abundance like we have never seen. Thousands of people arrived by the busloads to search for the boys. When they did locate them and discovered it was a desperate race against time to save them, people from all over the world threw themselves into the effort.

More than 200 expert cave divers flew in from England, Australia, China, Finland, and other lands to join the Thai Seals. Representatives from 200 agencies, including the United States, pitched in. Volunteers streamed in to cook meals, operate pumps, and provide medical assistance. Together, in a model of global cooperation almost inconceivable in our time, they did the impossible. Battling darkness, cold water, and powerful currents, the divers fought through grueling 11-hour trips to rescue the team. They got every one of the trapped children out alive. Everyone involved said it was a miracle. It was—a miracle proving that, spurred by compassion, we find far more resources among us than we ever knew existed. Given what happened there, I wonder how is it even possible that we allow any child in the world to go to bed hungry or homeless, claiming we don't have enough to do anything about it? It has all been exposed as an illusion.

That was the miracle, the magic, of the feeding of the five thousand. It is not a tale of a powerful, eccentric wizard conjuring bread out of thin air, dazzling the masses so that they will support him in his mission to take over the world. Jesus did not perform this amazing feat to impress or awe anyone. He was well aware that in doing what he did, he would only exacerbate the problem of the masses hounding him, favor-seekers stalking him, people trying to turn him into an earthly king.

But he did it anyway. He did it because he had compassion for people who were in need of food, of healing, of life. He gave them what they needed because that is what God is all about: sharing, healing, loving, giving life.

I'm pretty sure we have been given this story to show us that God has not created a world of scarcity; that's an illusion of our own making. We have been given far more than we need on this planet to feed everyone, to provide decent healthcare for everyone, to eradicate poverty and disease in this world, if only we act in compassion.

Chapter 9

I Wonder:
How does Jesus become wine and bread?

There has probably been no more divisive teaching in the Christian church than doctrines surrounding communion, also known as the Lord's Supper, or the eucharist. Throughout history, countless lives have been lost over this issue, and it continues to divide Christian denominations to this day.

I can't help but wonder what is going on in the sacrament of communion and why what was meant to be a unifying rite has instead torn the church away from its role as a healing, life-enhancing community. What is this sacrament really about, and is it worth all the trouble it has caused?

My wonderings have led me into the realm of banana slugs, of all places. In 1986, students at the University of California at Santa Cruz staged a fascinating revolt. The school was relatively new, having opened its doors in 1965. It had no history or tradition associated with a nickname or mascot for its athletic teams. At some point prior to that time, the administration arbitrarily designated them the "Sea Lions."

The student body did not want to be known as the Sea Lions. Over the opposition of the administration, they succeeded in putting the issue to a vote. The students' choice for school mascot crushed the Sea Lions by a whopping 15-to-1 margin. What made this election noteworthy was not so much the revolt as the choice of mascot. In a nation in which virtually every sports team chooses the symbol of a powerful or majestic beast, a fierce warrior, or imposing force of nature, the UC-Santa Cruz teams became known as the Banana Slugs.

People around the country assumed this was a prank or a joke. Why would anyone want to take on the image of a slow, slimy, defenseless, and in many people's minds, disgusting,

8-inch long mollusk? It seemed the students were making a mockery of their institution.

But, more than 30 years later, the UC-Santa Cruz sports teams are still known as the Banana Slugs. What's more, they take pride in that fact. The banana slug happens to be a key link in the ecosystem that produces the breathtaking Redwood forest that surrounds the campus. Despite appearances, it is a valuable little critter.

But even more importantly, the banana slug mascot makes a statement. It gives the school an identity that distinguishes it from all other higher academic institutions. Its selection stands as a symbol of the creative, independent, and adventurous spirit that has helped the university establish itself as a respected academic institution.

The Santa Cruz Banana Slug gives us some insight into the nature and importance of *symbols*. This is an important issue today because there is a large element of the faith community that downplays and even rejects the idea of symbolism in the Bible. Biblical literalism is a rejection of symbolism. People who are uncomfortable with wondering measure a person's faith by whether or not they accept symbols.

In this view, symbols are bad. A true Bible-believing Christian, a person of strong faith, is the one who accepts everything in the Bible as straight, unvarnished, clinical dictionary expression of the truth. Those who talk about symbols are weak, wavering in the faith. When you hear people say that the mainline churches are watering down the true intent of God's word and rejecting the authority of the Bible, what they are criticizing is the claim that the Bible relies heavily on symbols.

That is dangerous because symbols were at the heart of Jesus' ministry. The symbols he used were often difficult for people to grasp at first, but eventually enough listeners got it so that they could understand what his ministry was all about. I think it is safe to say they never would have gotten it without the symbols.

It follows that *we* would never understand what Jesus is all about without the symbols. Unless you recognize that Jesus is using symbols, and understand what those symbols mean, there is no way you can understand his ministry.

As evidence of that we need go no further than John, Chapter 6. In verse 35, Jesus makes this statement: "I am the bread of life." Taking the viewpoint that the most literal interpretation is the most faithful, here is what Jesus said: "I am a baked mixture of flour, water, and yeast with a high starch content but containing enough usable protein to be of nutritive value." Is there anyone who believes that? I don't think so, in which case we're left with only two options: 1) Jesus really was a baked mixture of flour, water, and yeast, and only our shameful lack of faith in the Bible keeps us from accepting that, or 2) Jesus is using the image of bread, not literally, but as a symbol.

A symbol is not a rhetorical trick meant to obscure or twist or compromise reality. A symbol is nothing more or less than a way to put an abstract thought or idea into a picture—a visual image that we can see and remember. Humans cannot communicate without symbols. Thoughts and ideas are slippery things. We are capable of holding only so much abstraction in our heads before it blows away like dust in the wind. Images are what help us hold ideas in place. Are Santa Cruz sports teams composed of actual banana slugs? Are yellow ribbons powerful magnetic charms that draw missing people back to their homes? Is that peculiar red, white, and blue design of stars and stripes an idol—do we pledge allegiance to a piece of cloth? No, these are symbols that stand for something—they cement into place ideas that are difficult to communicate or remember in any other way.

Why do you see crosses all over the place in a Christian church? Is it because we have a particular fondness for the letter 't'? Is it because we think that instruments of torture are appropriate decorative accessories? No, the cross stands for something—it cements into place the elusive idea that God could actually love us so much that God would be willing to come to earth in human form and die for us so that we could have life.

Symbols work. They are effective. Which is why, despite strange notions of the sanctity of literalism, Jesus seldom spoke in anything but symbols in the Gospel of John. *I am the Bread of Life, the True Vine, the Good Shepherd, the Lamb of God.* None of this is literal. They are all symbols; symbols we need in order to understand the ministry of Jesus and to hold it in place in our heads.

What crucial idea was Jesus bringing to us in this declaration that he is the Bread of Life? To get at this we first need to see to whom Jesus was talking.

The verse that precedes Jesus' statement on being the bread of life, gives us a clue. My seminary advisor, an expert on biblical Greek, informed me that this verse is most accurately translated, "Then some boats came from Tiberius, which was near the place where they had eaten the bread after the Lord had given thanks." In other words, this crowd, which had been present at the feeding of the five thousand, got in their boats and followed Jesus across the lake. These people were from Tiberius.

Tiberius was a major city on the northern side of the Sea of Galilee. It was a brand spanking new city built by the Jewish King Herod as his shining capital — it had been in existence for only about a decade when this story takes place. Herod patterned the city after the major cultural powers in the world, the Greeks and Romans. It was named, in fact, after the Roman emperor.

When the Chinese staged the Olympics in Beijing in 2008, they went all-out to show the world how state-of-the-art their country was. Tiberius was Herod's way of doing the same thing, of showing off his kingdom as modern and as up-to-date as any place in the world. He made a dumb mistake, however, the kind of mistake that happens when you get disconnected from your religious roots. He placed the city at the site of an ancient burial ground. In Hebrew culture, any contact with the dead made you unclean and so the people wanted nothing to do with the place. No one would live there.

Desperately afraid of the humiliation he would suffer if his showcase city ended up as a ghost town, Herod bribed people by offering free land and housing to anyone who would move to Tiberius. The population of the city, therefore, was largely made up of those who cared more about their own personal bottom line than they did about any community or religious traditions. They were apparently typical of urban masses in the Roman Empire, who could be easily bought off with freebies. Roman rulers often headed off political unrest with a free distribution of grain, which led to the famous remark by Cicero that all the people were interested in was "bread and circuses." The Tiberius crowd is in this camp. So when Jesus comes in with a major bread giveaway at the feeding of the five thousand, what is their reaction? "Here's the guy with the free bread. We love it! Go Jesus!"

The crowd declared they were ready to let Jesus take charge and they would gladly follow him, provided he kept up his end of the deal. "All you have to do is show us a sign," they said. "Something like, say, all the free bread in the wilderness in the old Moses stories?"

Wait a minute! They just got free bread in the wilderness, as in the old Moses stories. What more powerful sign could they ask for than the feeding of the five thousand? It appears they're not interested in a sign. What they are saying with a sly wink is, "Keep the free bread coming, keep us well fed, and we're on your side."

Now one of the aims of the kingdom of God that Jesus ushered in *is* to feed the hungry. But to Jesus that is a justice issue; what is happening with this crowd is not the same thing at all. What he is running into here is cynical scheming and selfishness. This crowd does not have a clue what Jesus is really about. How does Jesus get the point across to people who are just looking for more freebies?

He does it with a symbol and a play on words. He did not wake up that morning saying, "You know, I feel kind of like a loaf of bread today. That would be a perfect metaphor for what I'm doing." He did not come into the world with a philosophy based on bread. Until this moment, it probably had never occurred to him to compare himself to bread. The symbol of bread comes out of the conversation with the people of Tiberius. Jesus uses their own words and the image with which they are obsessed, the image of bread, to show them who he is and what he is about.

Bread at that time was what kept people alive, especially the masses. About two-thirds of the average diet at that time consisted of cereal grains, usually in the form of bread. Jesus is not discounting the importance of bread in keeping people alive. In fact, he uses that understanding of the life-giving nature of bread to explain what his ministry is all about.

"I have come to bring you life," he says, "Real life. The path you are on is not going to get you there. While bakery bread is important, there is a lot more to life than just eating to stay alive. That's animal level existence; human life is meant to be so much more than that. The bread you crave will feed your body but it will not feed your soul."

He then tells them, "I have something for you that can feed your soul in the same way that bread feeds your body. Call it bread for the soul. What I am offering is the life that God wants you to have. A life lived in the presence of a loving and righteous God, a life of peace and understanding, a life that reaps the joy of shared community with God and with fellow humans, and with all of creation."

"Wow," says the crowd in verse 34. "This sounds fantastic! Forget this other bread. If you've got some super bread that will do all that, hey, bring it on. Let's eat that stuff."

They are taking Jesus' words literally. In order to get them to understand that this is symbolic, Jesus has to get a little more blunt, a little more graphic.

"I am the bread," he says. "The bread of life from heaven come to bring you real life. Eternal life. As bread is what gives your physical body life, I am here to give life to your mind and your spirit."

Of course, the crowd still does not get it. Stuck in literal land, they get hung up on words and definitions. Jesus tries to sort it out for them. But they are so obstinate in their attitude that the argument goes nowhere.

Rather than going around in circles with these people, Jesus takes that image of bread and turns it into a symbol so powerful that it carries through his entire ministry right to the end, where it will shape Christian worship forever. He chooses a symbol that works in the same way as the banana slug—a symbol so utterly shocking and outlandish that you cannot mistake it for anything but a symbol. This symbol conveys in one graphic image that what Jesus offers is as important to sustaining the true spirit of life as bread is to sustaining the metabolic functions of life:

"Whoever eats my flesh and drinks my blood will have this life."

In the rest of the chapter, those who take this statement literally turn away from Jesus in disgust. Spiritually, they are going to starve in the wilderness. Those who understand his statement as a symbol clarifying how completely God offers himself to us for our benefit, follow Jesus, and in so doing get what they need to live as God intends.

We all know that there is more to life than simply existing. We sense that we were created to be more than a complex form of virus that exists just for the sake of existing and reproducing. Humans are created for something more.

Bread and water can keep our bodies alive, but what is it that keeps our spirits alive? How do we find meaning? What is it that lifts us to that higher plane of life shared with God Almighty?

For the Christian, the self-giving love of God, brought to us in the person of Jesus is what brings life. This love does not come to us in the form of a special wafer that produces instant happiness. It comes in the presence of Christ, which we receive as bread for the journey of life. Through the grace of God, Christian churches serve it up regularly in the Word and in the sacrament.

This use of symbols is a profound thing. We can get side-tracked into literal narrowness and wither in the spiritual wilderness. Or we can accept the invitation to come and be fed.

Chapter 10

I Wonder:
Why did Jesus have to suffer so much?

I have often had issues with the doctrine of atonement. In a nutshell, that doctrine starts with the claim that all humans are sinful and violate God's commandments. Justice demands that humans be held accountable for their actions and therefore must satisfy whatever punishment God imposes. Humans, however, fall into such a debt that they are incapable of paying it off. Nothing less than death would satisfy the demands of justice. Fortunately for all of humanity, a loving God sent Jesus into the world to pay the penalty for our sins. Jesus' task in life was to suffer the extreme agony and death that we deserve, thereby giving us eternal salvation.

My problems with this doctrine have to do with the fact that it pretty well trashes the concept of forgiveness and paints a portrait of God as well, cruel. I know for a fact that I love my children far too much to even consider subjecting them to torture and death regardless of what they might do. It seems absurd to imagine God as being less loving than me.

My wonderings have caused me to consider atonement doctrine in light of The Iliad, Homer's ancient story about the Trojan War, that was required reading in my college years. One fascinating part about the book is what it reveals about the theology of the times. As Homer tells it, this epic conflict was not so much a test of strength and will between Greeks and Trojans as it was a board game between two competing teams of gods — kind of a cosmic version of chess or Stratego or Risk, with humans as the little plastic playing pieces.

In Greek mythology, human life existed for entertainment purposes only — the gods' entertainment. There was no point in pretending you had any control over your life or a purpose other than to amuse the gods. If it pleased the gods to have you dead or happy or miserable, then that's what you were.

The really disturbing thing is that there was no purpose to the gods' lives either, other than to amuse themselves. The gods of ancient Greece were not particularly admirable beings. They could be mean, vindictive, selfish, petty. In this Trojan War competition, they cheated shamelessly. What did this say about the relationship between humans and the gods? There really was none. Sure, gods had their favorites among humans, but then we tend to have our favorite Monopoly token or favorite color cribbage peg, and there's no relationship there. People worshipped and praised the gods not because the gods were good or deserving but because they were powerful. Flattery worked on these vain deities and your only hope for a decent life was to use it to become a favorite token of one of the gods.

There was as huge a gap between the gods and humans as there is between a grandmaster and the chess pieces. The key to life for the religious Greeks was understanding and accepting the fact that the gods were privileged beings way up in the sky and humans were little game pieces down on the Earth. That's where each belonged, and that's the way it would always be.

As I have said before, we think of this as rather primitive religion, but the influence of the ancient Greeks on each of us is more powerful than we think. You hear it every day in religious circles:

This tragedy was God's will.

The Lord took her from us.

This disaster is God's punishment for sinful living.

Thank you, God, for giving us the riches and safety and security that other people don't have.

Everything happens for a reason, because it's all part of God's plan.

God doesn't give anyone more trouble or sorrow than they can handle.

If God brought you to it; God will bring you through it.

All of those statements are presented as if they were Christian; but they are not. That's all ancient Greek stuff—right out of *The Iliad*. When we do not work very hard at spirituality, and most of us don't, we slide back into primitive notions. When we lose our sense of wonder or questioning, we do not recognize the world we live in.

For many people today, the only differences between Christianity and Greek mythology are that God does not have any serious competition, and that our God is good, not devious. Lucky for us, or we would be in exactly the same boat as the Trojans and Greeks, playing out our meaningless existence, slaughtering each other for the sake of some divine competition.

For many, God is still that privileged being way up there in the mysterious cosmos, manipulating the little chess pieces from afar for his own entertainment. The feeling is that there exists a huge gap between God and us, and that's the way God likes it. What separates us from God is power and goodness. God has it, we don't. The key to life is understanding and accepting that God is spotlessly clean, way up in the sky, and we are down in the mud. That's where each belongs, and that's the way it will always be.

This was the mindset of the people of Jerusalem who welcomed Jesus on Palm Sunday. God lives far off in the pure, rarified air; humans live in the mud of sinfulness. They knew their place in the world back then. So when someone divine came into their midst, their job was to show that they knew their place. They worked hard to maintain that huge distance between God and humans.

Do you ever wonder why Christians walk around with palm branches on the Sunday that commemorates Jesus' triumphant entry into Jerusalem? Palm branches were not just decorations in biblical times. People did not just wave them like flags at a Memorial Day parade. They laid them on the road in front of Jesus. That was not the only thing they put on the road; they also spread out their coats. They laid their best coats on a dirty road to be trampled. Why did they do that?

There are stories from the days of European royalty about the proper etiquette for when the queen was walking around outside. If there was a patch of mud in the queen's path, which was often the case in an era before sidewalks and paved streets, a true and loyal subject was expected to take off his coat and place it over the mud so that the queen would not get her feet dirty. Everyone knew their place. The privileged queen was up there. She didn't belong in the dirt and the mud; that's where the rest of us lived.

The same thing happened in this Palm Sunday ride. The palm branches and the coats were placed on the road to cover the dirt. They were put there so that even the beast upon which Jesus rode would not have to touch the dirt and the mud.

They proclaimed him the Messiah—the Savior, and the very presence of God. In their gestures with the palm branches and their coats, the crowd was saying, "We know our place. We know your place. We know you don't belong down in our world. It's shocking enough that you would even make an appearance in our dirty, sinful world. The least we can do is limit your contact with the dirt."

If Jesus behaved the way divine beings are supposed to behave, according to mythology, he would have accepted this as his due. "Excellent! You little mud dwellers know your place. Because of that I will be merciful to you and allow you to live. Don't expect me to get involved in your lives, though. As if I could get involved with playing pieces. As long as you keep treating me with the requisite respect, I'll let you enjoy some benefits and blessings that you don't deserve, just because it amuses me to allow this to happen. So, carry on."

That way was open to Jesus. And according to virtually all other societies in the world, that was the path he should have taken. There really was no choice. Humans belong in the mud;

the divine does not. Never the two shall mix. Greek mythology is filled with the tragic lessons of those humans who try to usurp the privilege of the divine.

In the Palm Sunday accounts, though, Jesus does the unimaginable. He does what the gods have warned against from the dawn of time. He does not know his place. He does not accept the huge barrier between God and human. After this ride through town, he gets down off the animal, kicks aside the palm branches and coats, and gets into the mud of the Garden of Gethsemane, of the palaces of Pilate and Herod, and on the hill of Golgotha.

To anyone who thinks that all world religions are basically the same, the story of Palm/Passion Sunday offers stunning evidence to the contrary. It turns all previously accepted ideas of religion on their heads. The reason I believe the Christian message is so important and needs to be proclaimed is not because it prescribes a code of behavior. You don't need religion to do that, much less Christianity—there are codes of behavior everywhere.

The insight that the Bible reveals is that God is far different from what humanity has imagined. God is not a privileged being who sits up in the clouds and avoids all contaminating contact with humans, whom he has created for his own amusement and entertainment. God created us for an entirely different reason—to share the gift of relationship. And in order to do that, God is willing to meet us where we live, down in the mud.

That truth is declared in the beautiful hymn recorded in Philippians 2. In the modern translation of *The Message* version of the Bible:

Jesus Christ did not think so much of himself that he had to cling to the advantages of that status. When the time came, he set aside the privileges of a deity and took on the status of a slave, became human. Having become human, he stayed human. It was an incredibly humbling process. He did not claim special privileges. Instead, he lived a selfless, obedient life and then died a selfless, obedient death—and the worst kind of death at that—a crucifixion.

That is not the kind of behavior we expect from the divine. That is loser behavior, and the world scoffs at it. But once it is explained to us, it is so beautiful and so logical, it's hard to see that God could be any other way. Would God's ultimate purpose be to preside over a collection of playing pieces? What kind of shallow existence is that? You can worship a God like that out of self-preservation instincts but you can't love that God. You can hardly even respect that God.

But what if God's purpose was to share love with as many other beings as possible? The Bible makes this claim. If that is true, then there is no way God sits far off on an antiseptic throne, manipulating what goes on in the universe without getting God's hands dirty. A God truly interested in sharing love is going to come down into the mud where we are floundering and choking and suffocating, and pull us out of it.

That is the unique message of Christianity.

The strongest evidence of the truth of this message is that we feel the presence of God most strongly when we see people imitating this mud-slogging characteristic of God.

Habitat for Humanity was a small, struggling enterprise when it first began. Do you remember when it grabbed the nation's consciousness and swelled into a huge movement with branches all across the country? It was about the time when people discovered former U.S. president Jimmy Carter quietly showing up every day in a work shirt and jeans to pound nails to help build a house for someone in need. In the unskilled labor of a powerful man of privilege, who had no need ever to go into the mud again, we saw a clear reflection of God.

It's no fun changing dirty diapers, or cleaning up after an aged person who no longer has control over bodily functions. But there are few acts of love as pure and honorable as those.

Several years ago, there was a devastating mudslide in La

Conchita California. A 30-foot wall of mud slammed into a neighborhood in this small mountain community. It swallowed up houses and killed ten people.

Listen to excerpts of an interview with one of the residents of La Conchita Bill Harbison, who happened to be out riding his bike in the neighborhood when the mountainside came down: "I just jumped in—calling out for people—climbing through the mud and all the wreckage."

Harbison heard the voices of two women trapped deep in the mud, about 25 feet apart. He remembers pulling one of them out and, as he says, "I put her on my back and carried her out piggyback. I handed her off and then jumped back in the mud. I dug and dug and finally found the second woman." She was alive only because she was in a little pocket of air that kept her from being suffocated.

"I got down to her, and was actually able to look her in the eye—make eye contact and hold her hand and say, 'I'm here. We're not going to leave you. We're going to get you out.'" He stayed with her, holding on to her until help arrived and the woman was rescued.

Read the Passion story and you will see Jesus kick aside the palm branches and the coats, and jump into the mud to save a floundering humanity trapped and suffocating in its own selfishness and sin and hatred. Watch as he gets down on his knees and digs down with his bare hands into the mess that we have made of the world. Watch as he slogs waist-deep through the mud of human failure on the way to the cross, and when he gets there, he looks us in the eye, holds our hand, and says, "I'm here. I'm not going to leave you. I'm going to get you out." Watch as he stays with us to the bitter end until help finally arrives, and he does get us out.

The ancient Greeks were incredibly wise and learned in many ways. But they knew nothing about God. They could never have imagined, much less written, these words from Philippians:

Christ Jesus did not consider equality with God something to be grasped, but made himself nothing, taking the very nature of a servant, being made in human likeness. *And being found in appearance as a man, he humbled himself and became obedient to death — even death on a cross.*

That is the story that Christians are given to tell the world. This is what we believe God is really like. That is why we in the Lutheran church do not celebrate Palm Sunday without also celebrating Passion Sunday. Because, while I am sure he appreciated the gesture, Jesus did not want the palms. He was not concerned with staying clean. He wanted to help us, and he was willing to go as far into the mud as necessary to reach us.

Chapter 11

I Wonder:
Can a person really rise from the dead?

At the heart of the Christian message is a lot of fuss about an Easter miracle, and from people we normally consider sane and level-headed. Jesus died and came back to life, huh? Looking at this objectively and rationally, that makes no sense. Dead people do not come back to life: unless you believe in miracles.

I'm not big on miracles. Miracles do not make sense, scientifically or in my understanding of God. They don't even make sense mathematically. The fact is, if the odds are a million to one against something happening, every time it happens, we claim it's a miracle, breaking the laws of nature. But in reality, that event is occurring with exactly the frequency that science said it would. So, no, I'm not big on miracles.

Now, before you drag me off and stone me, let's be clear on what I'm talking about. I am using a strict definition of the word "miracle," as in "violent intervention with natural law." Yes, we call the birth of a child a miracle. We call it a miracle when someone suddenly turns their life around, or has a powerful vision of God. We call the way the Holy Spirit dramatically stirs people, provides healing, and influences the lives of believers "miracles." And, yes, many things happen in our world that science cannot explain. I am aware that there are far more clouds than there are clocks in the universe.

None of this is what I mean by miracle. The Easter story does not talk about stuff that is merely awesome, or inspiring, or puzzling. It describes a miracle defined as *a case where the rules of nature are dramatically sabotaged.* Like dead people coming back to life. I'm skeptical about that kind of miracle.

I am skeptical of miracles because the evidence of all creation is that God loves order and logic and rational thought. God made a world governed by those principles. God built the universe on a system of unbreakable laws because that is the kind of world that God wanted to make. That must be the kind of world that expresses who God is. If God wanted to make a magical world, where the rules change at the snap of a finger, where you chant a few notes and voila! winter turns to spring, God could have done that. But God didn't.

We keep trying to push that kind of a world on God because we think that would be a big improvement on the flawed world that God has made. But we have not thought it through. God made the world orderly and rational because God is faithful. God's nature does not change; it is not subject to whims. Because God is faithful, you can count on creation being what it is. You can drive across a bridge over the Mississippi River without a second's worry that the rules of engineering that built that bridge are fluid and the whole thing may vanish into thin air. When you travel in an airplane, you know the laws of physics that held that plane up yesterday are on the job today and will hold it up.

We plant crops in full confidence that the seed will grow into a plant just like the one that produced it. We bet our lives that photosynthesis is a reality we can count on. We know that the process by which the human body chemically breaks down food into forms that keep us alive is not just something that worked in the past but might not this time. It's going to be there.

God's faithfulness helps us know our limits. We do not jump out of airplanes without a parachute on a hunch that the laws of gravity just might go our way this time. We know what gravity will do, every second of every day, and so we account for it in our plans. You could come up with a thousand examples of this faithfulness.

Short-sighted people that we are, we do not stop to think how lucky we are that God is reluctant to surrender faithfulness in favor of miracles. When a parent develops Alzheimer's, or a loved one contracts a fatal or crippling disease, or ends up in a perilous situation, we don't like it, and we are quick to throw in the towel. We want God to scrap the world God so lovingly and painstakingly made, and suddenly create a new, magical, temporary one for our personal benefit. We convince ourselves that God is the kind of being who says, "The laws of the universe that I made will apply to the million people who will die in the world today, but if you pray nicely, I'll make an exception just for you."

Although it seems terribly callous when we are in dire need or confronted with tragedy, it is a good thing that God does not go in big for miracles. If we lived in a world filled with miracles, nothing would make sense. We could count on nothing, could plan for nothing. We could not be responsible or moral beings because God could just snap God's fingers and fix all the consequences of our actions.

If God wanted to create a world in which rules do not matter, God could have done that. But God did not. God made the rules that govern creation. For God to perform miracles then, God has to break God's own rules. God has to fight against God, and that makes no sense.

So I really wonder about miracles.

That being the case, what do I do with the powerful testimony from witnesses that there was an empty tomb—that they saw Jesus risen? This event was so real and powerful to them that almost overnight it changed the disciples from a bunch of confused, timid rabbits into the most powerful evangelizing force the world has ever seen. They were so certain the impossible happened that they stuck to their story even when it meant suffering and death.

How does a wonderer like me, who says miracles don't make sense, deal with that? For me, it turns out there is an interesting answer close by, in the lakes that surround us in my part of the world. Because they contain one of the biggest miracles you will ever witness, in the strict definition of the word.

As water cools, the molecules contract and the water becomes denser. Water at 180 degrees F is denser than water at 200 degrees. Water at 99 is denser than water at 100. Water at 70 is denser than water at 71. It is an absolutely predictable, verifiable pattern of nature. A line on a graph. No exceptions.

So, what would you predict would happen when water hits 36 degrees? It would be denser than water at 37, right? It's not. The pattern does not just change; it does not just stop and begin to reverse course; that would be unusual but plausible within the rules of science and logic. No, it grinds to a halt and then, magically, it jumps off the chart. When water hits 32 degrees it inexplicably becomes less dense than even 200-degree water. In short, a miracle (a dramatic sabotage of nature) happens.

So God does make exceptions to the rules!

Why this exception? I cannot presume to read God's mind, but I can observe one result of this miracle. It makes life possible on a vast scale.

In a winter climate, if water did not suddenly take a huge, irrational, miraculous jump to the other side of the density chart, what would happen when ice formed on the surface of a lake in winter? It would sink to the bottom. Colder means denser; denser sinks. You would have a cycle in which water on the surface is constantly freezing and sinking, freezing and sinking. By mid-January every lake in a northern climate would be frozen solid from top to bottom, killing every living thing in it.

Thank God that the bizarre science that takes place with water does not happen often, because if it did, the world would be too weird for us to do anything with. There would be no science, no medicine, no engineering, you name it. But this rare exception makes possible on a vast scale life that would not exist otherwise.

God does not save life in the lakes by constantly breaking into the world to miraculously save one fish at a time, in one lake at a time, every time it gets cold. God saved life by accomplishing one rare miracle that saves all the fish in all the lakes for all time.

In view of that, what happened at the empty tomb on Easter morning begins to make sense. Nature-defying miracles are not something God routinely does for lucky individuals, one at a time, in place after place, day after day. In the Easter story, God performed a miracle, once, for all people, for all time. God seldom deals in miracles, because to do so is for God to act against God's own rules. And that is hard and painful and costly for God to do.

Yes, God can do miracles. But do you think miracles are easy and cheap? Then if all God needed to do to put us right with the world was to snap God's fingers, why did Jesus suffer and die on a cross? To perform a miracle, God has to fight against God, and that comes at a steep price.

If you take miracles for granted, like God does them all the time and can do them whenever God wants, then Easter is a fun holiday, filled with chocolate bunnies and jellybeans, but it isn't special. Then the Easter resurrection is just another cool trick and God's got a million of them in the bag and can pull them out any time God feels like it.

I cannot say why God loved us enough to come into our world and suffer death, followed by the miracle of resurrection; but I can observe the result. It makes life possible on a vast scale. Eternal life, beginning with life here on earth.

Do we have to believe the impossible to be Christians? For the most part, no. God interacts with the world in many ways, but generally leaves science alone, because the natural world is God's creation and God is faithful to it. To paraphrase John Polkinghorne, too many Christians believe that faith means clenching your fists and gritting your teeth and believing as many impossible things as you can because some religious authority says you have to.

But according to John 3:16, real Christianity is opening your heart and letting go, and believing *one* impossible thing. That God so loved the world that he paid a horrific price to break

God's own rules: Jesus was sent to his death, and then raised from the dead so that whoever believes in him will have eternal life.

"That whoever believes?" Isn't that a little exclusive? Why is it so important that we believe something unbelievable? Couldn't a loving God just give the miracle of life to everyone no matter what they happen to think? Yes. But remember that God created science and logic. And the logic is simple: you cannot accept a gift from someone if you do not believe in the existence of the gift or the giver. The gift is yours only when you come to believe that the gift exists. If you do not believe that God could raise Jesus from the dead, then you do not believe God could do it for you. If the story of Easter cannot be true, then, logically, you can only conclude that when that last shovelful of dirt covers your casket, you're done. You're gone forever. Your life is without hope.

If you believe that God broke the rules on death once, for all time, for everyone, including you, then your life is changed, you have so much to look forward to. Now you just might be ready to celebrate this incredible miracle we call Easter.

Part III

Questions about Spirits

Chapter 12

I Wonder:
What exactly is the Holy Spirit?

If you have ever wanted to say to an ordained minister, regarding an issue of theology, "you don't know what you're talking about," this is a golden opportunity for you. Because this chapter centers on the Holy Spirit, and I will be the first to confess I don't know much about spirits, holy or otherwise.

There are people who do. I spent some time on the Pine Ridge Reservation in South Dakota. There I got to know a Lakota woman who told me a story of her encounter with a spirit. The sharing of such a vision is deeply personal, even sacred, to a Lakota, and so to this day I do not share details. All I can tell you is that her story was so vivid and detailed, so terrifying and so real, it made the hairs on my neck stand on end.

I will admit, I did not know exactly what to make of her story. What she told me was so far outside of my realm of experience that I didn't know how to respond except simply to listen, be amazed, and wonder.

Then, many years later, I had an encounter with the spirit realm. As my father lay dying, I periodically read passages from the Bible that I knew meant something to him. The last one I chose was from Revelation 21. As I stood beside his bed reading those verses, suddenly a feeling came over me that I cannot describe. The best I can say is that it felt like something was moving within me and flowing through me—not through my mind but through my body—gathering energy and then releasing it. I looked at Dad and discovered that he had passed into death at the exact moment this was happening.

Again, I do not know what to make of it except to simply be amazed and wonder at this experience, of a power and a depth of meaning that I can barely begin to comprehend. I am guessing that most people are as unfamiliar as I am with the subject of spirits. After all, spirits are not a big part of twenty-first-century American culture, except as characters in horror flicks. When it comes to spirits, most of us cannot begin to sort out where superstition ends and reality begins. And if we are baffled by talk of spirits, it stands to reason that we are equally uncomfortable with talk of a Holy Spirit.

That creates a problem for a lot of Christians because we are taught that the Holy Spirit is an essential element of the Christian faith. When we baptize, we do so in the name of the Father, the Son, and the Holy Spirit. Our faith statement includes a belief in the Trinity, God in three persons, one of which is the Holy Spirit. In our creeds we proclaim, "I believe in the Holy Spirit."

So what does it mean to believe in the Holy Spirit? Do we have any idea of what we are talking about when we say that? What is this Holy Spirit we say that we believe in? Can you describe it? Can you define it?

If we are having trouble with this, it's not surprising, since the New Testament, the main source of our information on the Holy Spirit, cannot pin it down either. As far as I can tell, the New Testament never comes close to either a clear definition or description. The Gospels say that, after Jesus was baptized, the Holy Spirit descended "as a dove." And so artists for centuries have portrayed the Holy Spirit as a dove. But that's not what the passage says. The text says, "the Spirit descended like a dove." In other words, I can't tell you what it is, but something about the way it descends reminds me of the way a dove would descend.

The book of Acts says that at Pentecost the Spirit came down "with a sound like a strong wind." It then goes on to say that it appeared to them "like tongues of fire." Again, artists have taken this and depicted the Holy Spirit as fire. But that's not what the Bible says. It says that something appeared, and the closest way it can be described is that it was kind of like a flame.

Taken altogether, here is how the New Testament describes

the Holy Spirit. "It descends kind of like a dove, and it reminds one in some ways of a blast of wind or a dancing flame." If that sounds clear to you, just imagine putting out an APB that reads, "Be on the lookout for something that moves kind of like a dove and reminds you of a gust of wind or maybe a flame." If someone says that to me, my reaction is, "You don't really know what you're talking about, do you?"

In trying to describe what the Holy Spirit is, I wonder if the New Testament writers really knew what they were talking about. I suspect they would admit that they did not, and from my experience, I am not surprised.

Part of their problem is the difficulty of the subject and part of it is the language they are writing in. They are using Greek, and Greek is the language of logic, the language of science. It is precise, fact-oriented. And when you're using logical, scientific, precise, fact-oriented language to describe a spirit, you are not going to get very far.

If we really want to understand spirit, we need to use a language that is more comfortable communicating in pictures, images, and story. Hebrew, the language of the Old Testament, is such a language, and it might be a good idea to look there for an understanding of spirit.

The Hebrew word for Holy Spirit is "ruah". Psalm 51 says "Cast me not away from your presence and take not your ruah [Holy Spirit] from me."

The Hebrew word for Spirit of God is "ruah" Job 33:4 says, "The ruah [Spirit of God] has made me, and the breath of the Almighty gives me life." The Hebrew word for wind from God is "ruah." Genesis 1:2 reads, "darkness covered the face of the deep while a ruah [wind from God] swept over the face of the waters."

The Hebrew word for the atmospheric condition that we know as wind is "ruah." Ezekiel 1:4 says, "As I looked, behold, a stormy ruah [wind] came out of the north."

The Hebrew word for "unseen presence" is (big surprise) "ruah." In II Kings 5, Elisha asks, "Was I not there with you in ruah [in spirit, in unseen presence]?"

The word is identical in all cases. Hebrew does not try to make a distinction between wind, spirit, Holy Spirit, wind from God, unseen mortal presence, God's Spirit. They are all part of the same invisible, indescribable but very real and recognizable presence in our world.

We can understand that presence by looking at the part of ruah which is most accessible to us: wind. Wind is one of those things with which everyone is familiar, but almost no one knows what it really is. If you want to be New Testament Greek about it, wind is defined as the result of a variance of barometric pressure in the atmosphere. Wind is air pulled from an area of high pressure into an area of low pressure. Technically, wind does not blow, it sucks.

Knowing the definition of wind, however, tells you almost nothing about it. A three-year-old child can tell you far more about wind than a pile of charts filled with isobars.

Wind is that which brings a moment of glorious cool relief on a sweltering summer day. It is that which teases the waves out of the flat surface of a lake, that holds up a kite or a hawk high in the sky, that strips leaves off trees in autumn, that turns a routine fly ball into a home run, that freezes your face when it's cold, that whisks a dollar bill out of your hands and makes you chase it down the street, that stirs up a dust cloud, or causes a wildfire to explode.

A true understanding of wind has nothing to do with a technical explanation of what wind is; it has everything to do with experience of what wind does.

I have come to believe that the same is true of the Holy Spirit. An explanation of what the Holy Spirit is, is virtually worthless, if it is even possible. The Spirit is the unseen, indescribable but very real presence of God in our world. We know the Spirit of

God by experiencing what the Spirit does.

What is it, then, that the Holy Spirit does? In his book, *Through Seasons of the Heart,* John Powell describes some ways that the Holy Spirit acts on us. I'll focus briefly on four:

1. The Spirit acts on our emotions. This is the action most traditionally associated with spirit. It's that old, "We've got spirit, yes we do, we've got spirit, how about you?" Spirit is something we feel. Where does the concept of joy come from, if not from the Spirit? Where does the notion of beauty come from, if not the Spirit? When I feel lonely, or pessimistic, or upset, or angered, or embittered, what pulls me out of it?

The Spirit of God can dissolve the hatred that consumes me, cut the chains of sadness that drag me down, calm the anxiety that paralyzes me. The Spirit can take the love that constantly pours forth from God and apply it to our broken and wounded selves where we need it the most. The Gospel of John, despite being written in Greek, follows the Hebrew example of defining the Holy Spirit by what it does, not by what it is when it refers to it as the Comforter: I don't know what it is, but I know what it does—it comforts.

2. Second, the Holy Spirit acts on our minds. I am a firm believer that God assists the flow of ideas into people's heads. I cannot tell you how many times I have been writing a book, article, or sermon when all of a sudden, an idea pops into my head and I can't help but wonder, "where did that come from?" I know the answer, and it is not that I was so clever as to figure it all out on my own. Sometimes the Spirit of God helps you say what you need to say. I believe the spirit of God is acting in the world whenever new ideas or visions come into being that benefit creation.

I believe the spirit of God helps us to make decisions. Whenever we wrestle, individually or as a group, with issues, ideas, and choices, the spirit of God is available to us to help in that process. That is what Jesus means when he refers to the

Holy Spirit as the Counselor.

3. Third, the Holy Spirit acts on our will. This is more than just a matter of giving us the willpower to resist temptation and sin. As Powell puts it, "more than simply steeling my will to the challenge of costly discipleship, God's spirit has come to me in prayer and put into my will new desires." The Spirit makes me want to be a better person. It makes me want to give more of myself to God's work. I am sure that every great accomplishment in all of human history began with the birth of a desire in some human heart. And I know where that desire comes from—from the Spirit of God.

4. Finally, the Holy Spirit acts on our memory. It reminds us time and again of what God has done in the past, how God acted in the lives of the faithful throughout history. And in so doing, it grows faith. Faith that helps us believe the promises God has made to us for the future. It is a gift of the Holy Spirit to prod our memories to stir up those feelings of love, appreciation, and insight.

Whenever someone says, "I have never forgotten what my father did that time when I needed..."

Or "I've never forgotten when our car broke down on that country road and this stranger helped us by..."

Or, "I've never forgotten how God's comfort carried me through that terrible time when..."

Or, "I've never forgotten that Sunday School teacher who took the time to..."

Or "I've never forgotten that time when the members of this congregation came through for me when I really needed it..."

When you remember these things, you are feeling the wind of God blowing across the face of the earth.

The Holy Spirit does not solve all problems or give all answers, or write books or sermons for that matter. It is not a magic power to be summoned at our command or made to perform for us. The Holy Spirit has no interest in bailing out preachers too lazy to prepare thoughtfully for a sermon, or writers, accountants, teachers, nurses, or farmers too lazy to work at the skills of their craft, students too lazy to study for tests, leaders too timid to make decisions, or narrow-minded people expecting divine backing for their prejudices.

As best as I can understand it, this Spirit *is* available as a valuable resource to those who open themselves to its power. Just as the Spirit of God swept over the universe at creation, that Spirit swept over Jesus at his baptism. That Spirit sweeps over us at our baptism and makes us God's children; and is active and sweeping over the face of the earth today.

Chapter 13

I Wonder:
Is demon possession a real thing?

When I began serving at my first congregation, we had all kinds of problems with the computers—in my office and in the church office. As soon as one problem was cleared up, another would appear—sometimes with email, sometimes with memory, sometimes with the system locking up. For seemingly no reason, and at random times, the computer simply did not do what it was supposed to do. This resulted in what the Bible would call gnashing of teeth and a great deal of wasted time.

At one point, after yet another setback, frustration reached such a peak that I suggested we look into performing an exorcism on the computers. Of course, I was not seriously contemplating that as an option. It was merely a reflection of the bewilderment and frustration we felt at being thwarted at every turn by these computers. It almost seemed as though there was a diabolical presence in the machines that was determined to ruin our work.

Okay, shame on me for making light of a subject as serious as demon possession. But if you read the medical and psychiatric journals and textbooks, and attend counseling seminars, you don't find a great deal of information on demon possession. Health care professionals are not in the habit of diagnosing patients as being possessed by evil spirits, nor do they commonly prescribe exorcism as the cure. There are no demon-possession specialists on staff at any clinic or hospital that I know.

We do hear about violent criminals who claim to have heard voices in their heads, demonic voices telling them to commit terrible deeds. But the criminally insane are as likely to claim that it was the voice of God telling them to kill as they are to insist it was a demon, which makes the whole thing suspect.

Back in Jesus' time, there appear to have been demons all

over the place, causing all sorts of evil. I have to wonder; how do we explain the huge influence of demons back then compared to their marginalized status today? Where have all the demons gone? Do they exist? Did they ever exist? There seem to be four possible answers to that question. The least plausible is that the world was crawling with demons in Jesus' time but those beings have pretty well disappeared from the world today. It's hard to imagine that demons once thrived and now, for some unknown reason, have gone the way of the dinosaurs. I have never seen anyone argue that some environmental or behavioral factor has put demons on the endangered species list.

A second answer is that references to demons in the Bible are a result of the limited understanding of science at that time. There is certainly some truth to this. People in biblical times knew little about the causes of illness.

They noticed a connection between pork and illness, which may account for some of the dietary laws in the Old Testament. But they would have been astounded to learn that the world is filled with invisible microbes that are responsible for disease. They knew nothing of chemical imbalances that affect behavior, or of the intricate nature of the electrical grid in the brain. They had no idea that biological malfunctions in nervous system activity could produce an epileptic seizure. Lacking rational explanations for the sudden appearance and sometimes disappearance of strange behavior and deadly diseases, they had little choice but to attribute these occurrences to the influence of unseen forces. The sheer destruction caused by these health failures would certainly steer people in the direction of labeling these unseen forces as evil, demonic.

It could be, in fact is likely, that in some of the biblical stories of healing through the exorcism of demons, people misunderstood what was happening in medical terms. It is no coincidence that widespread focus on demons continued through the Middle Ages, through the Renaissance, right up to the time that the age of science pulled back the curtain on what is really going on in the natural world.

A third explanation for the demon gap is that our culture is so materialistic, fact-oriented and logic-oriented that we have lost access to the spiritual world. In clinically treating symptoms without regard to the spiritual realities, we in the modern world are the ones who are blind and ignorant.

There is certainly some truth to that. Most of the medical community has come to realize that there is more to healing than prescribing the right pills. The best approach to overall health is a holistic one that involves taking care of one's mental and spiritual health. In many ways we have returned to the wisdom of older cultures, including that of biblical times, that have long known that health and happiness can best be achieved by restoring balance and equilibrium with the world in which we live.

Furthermore, tragic events around the world have destroyed the smug modern assertion that there is no such thing as evil in the world—that there are only mistakes and ignorance, bad choices and bad information. We have seen evil in our time and have trembled at its ferocity. The staggering cold-bloodedness of the Nazi holocaust. The brutality of ethnic cleansing that rears its ugly head again and again. The never-ending cycle of perverting religious doctrines into blueprints for terrorism. The demented glare of the serial killer who sits in a courtroom showing not an ounce of remorse. The lowlife drug lord without a conscience who builds a life of luxury by destroying lives of the young and gullible.

Those are not just mistakes and bad choices. There is something else going on. People who dabble in the occult as a joke often find that there's more there than they bargained for, and it is terrifying. There are powers at work in the world; powers that scare us. We cannot put our finger on what these forces are, or how they come to be, how they grow and consume and destroy, but we know they are real.

I do not pretend to be able to resolve all the issues and questions regarding mental and physical health and demons and forces of evil. What my wondering about this issue has caused me to do is propose a way of looking at this issue that will bring us what the Bible intends to bring us: new life lived in the light of the God of love and justice.

I propose that we combine answers 2 & 3, and begin by separating the truth that the Bible reveals about demon possession from the rather primitive understanding of health issues at the time. What happened in the story from Luke where Jesus encountered the demoniac? We can say only this with certainty: Jesus met a fellow who was seriously ill, probably criminally insane. The only explanation available at the time for behavior so terrifying and bizarre was that he was possessed by demons. The only treatment they knew of was to put him in chains so he could not hurt anyone when these violent fits of insanity took hold of him.

The diagnosis would be different today, and the treatment would be different, but that does not change the situation that confronted Jesus. Here was a man who could no longer take responsibility for his actions. His life was dominated by a force beyond his control. And whatever you want to call that outside force, the effect on his life was certainly demonic.

We know that humans were not meant to live that way. We were not designed by our creator to be controlled by destructive forces outside of us. We were not meant to live enslaved by forces of evil. We were meant to live free and responsible for our lives in the light and grace of God, to draw strength and healing from God's love and to reflect that love. Yet there are forces in this world that co-opt us, that corrupt us, that enslave and control us. Are these forces actual beings? They could be, but they don't have to be. Evil is a force and forces do not require individual identity or even consciousness.

Back to computers. I clearly remember a time in the early days of computers in the 1970s when I experienced the presence of evil in these machines. My college aquatic biology class was assigned to use a computer to analyze some data. Back in those days, computers were so far from user-friendly it wasn't funny. You had to type in reams of code instructions to get the computer to do anything.

These instructions had to be incredibly precise. If you made the tiniest error in entering any of these many instructions, the computer would type out three question marks. It would never tell you what you did wrong or needed to change. Just a cold, impersonal ??? I once spent an entire evening trying to get the instructions right, and all I ever got for my efforts were these ???

Eventually I got so mad at the computer it was all I could do to keep from ramming the keyboard through the monitor. The machine was so heartless, so indifferent to humanity, so smug, so arrogant. I was trying my best. I was exhausted and desperate, and it just mocked me with those stupid question marks. I don't know that I have ever been any angrier at a human being than I was at that inanimate object. I was bursting with hatred for that computer, wanting nothing more than to smash it into a thousand pieces.

Impulses of hatred and destruction are forces of evil. I experienced this demonic force, felt it grow until it very nearly controlled me. And what created this evil force? An object that had no identity, no consciousness. Forces do not need individual identity or even consciousness. An impulse of hatred and destruction becomes demon possession when it controls you, when you become like the sick man in the gospel story who is powerless to resist it.

The author C.S. Lewis had a similar experience. He wrote a book called *The Screwtape Letters* from the point of view of a senior devil mentoring a junior demon. When asked to write a sequel to this bestseller, Lewis refused. The experience of writing the first book had left him shaken. Just putting himself inside the character of a being filled with such malice and spite damaged his spiritual health, his sense of well-being. Never again would he open himself up to that influence. He felt the power of evil and its power to control and he wisely put distance between himself and that power.

My computer experience, combined with Lewis's experience, has cautioned me against trying to pinpoint or define the nature of demonic forces. All I know is that they exist, and they are deadly. When they take root in us, they tend control us—to rob us of the freedom of living as God intended.

In Western civilization, we have come to recognize, albeit belatedly, that slavery is a sin against God and creation. It is simply wrong to own another person. Being owned by another person means they control what you do, and so assume all the responsibilities and privileges of your life. In effect, they subsume your life. It is bad enough to be owned by another person, but slavery becomes especially tragic when the slave owner is evil, when he mistreats the slaves, causes great suffering, pain, and death.

In the story of the demoniac, Jesus comes face to face with a person who is not in control of his life. The man is a slave to his illness. He is owned by a force beyond his control or understanding, and that force is evil. It causes great suffering, pain, and ultimately, death. You can view that force anyway you want; you can personify it or not. What matters is that it controls him and it is evil.

Jesus comes to him and gives him back his life. He releases him from the grip of the demonic force so that he is free to live in the light and life that God intended. That's what Jesus does. That's why Jesus came.

The questions I came to ask myself were "what are my personal demons? What has me in its grip and steers me in directions I do not want to go, or should not go? What is it in me that causes grief and hardship in my life? What is it in me that causes grief and hardship in the lives of those around me? What is it in me that fans the flames of hatred and violence? What has me in its control that prevents me from being the person I know God intended me to be?"

Evil is a powerful force in the world, and none of us is immune to its influence. Christians acknowledge this when we repeat the prayer that our Lord taught us to pray. The plea for God to "Deliver us from evil," is as heartfelt today as it was 2000 years ago.

The Gospel declares that Jesus came to free us from the control of the forces of evil, in whatever form that evil takes. To give us our lives back again. It is what we call salvation.

Chapter 14

I Wonder:
Is speaking in tongues really a thing?

In college, I lived in a dorm room next to a guy who was very much into speaking in tongues. Occasionally during the year, I could hear him through the thin walls, shouting and spluttering what sounded to me like complete gibberish. For many years, I wondered what that was all about, and how what I heard related to the claim in the Bible that speaking in tongues was a gift of the Holy Spirit. It has been a long and difficult journey, and the fact remains that I still have no experience of anything remotely close to what people call glossolalia.

The most influential stop on my journey was at the tower of Babel. The tower of Babel story is an ancient fable, told from the perspective of the very limited anthropological and engineering knowledge of the time. The story tells of a world in which all people speak only one language. A group of men decide to build a great city with a tower that reaches to the heavens, "so that they may make a great name for themselves."

The Lord comes down to look at the construction project and does not like what is going on. "If as one people speaking the same language they have begun to do this, then nothing they plan to do will be impossible for them." God appears to be concerned that they will succeed in their task of building a tower to the heavens, and that in so doing they will then be able to take over God's role in the world.

In this story, the Lord responds by making them all speak in tongues, in different languages. No one can understand what the other is saying. This disrupts their communications and makes any cooperative effort impossible. Their plan is foiled. They are unable to complete their fabulous tower. They are scattered across the earth, where they are no longer a threat. God's place in the universe is saved.

Is this supposed to be a report of an historical event? That's an easy question to answer with some elementary logic. Prior to 1884 the tallest structure ever built in the entire course of human history, the Great Pyramid of Cheops, topped out at 481 feet. Not exactly up in the heavens. Would anyone seriously suggest that the reason buildings were no taller through those thousands of years until almost the end of the nineteenth century was because of language issues?

As of this writing, the tallest human-made building currently in existence is the Burj Khalifa in Dubai. Completed on October 1, 2009, it towers over all other human-made structures at 2717 feet, more than twice as tall as New York's Empire State building. Ask any engineer if people in ancient biblical times, all speaking the same language, could have built a tower that high with the materials and technology available.

Even if we suspend reason and concede they could have built such a tower in olden times, would this have been remotely threatening to God? Consider these four facts:

1) As spectacular as it looks to us from the ground floor, the Dubai building is not even visible in a satellite image of the Earth.
2) The Earth is 1/100th the size of the star it orbits—the sun.
3) There are more stars in God's universe than there are grains of sand in the largest beach in the world.
4) The boundaries of the universe are at least 100,000,000,000,000,000,000 miles apart.

These facts show that, in the scope of the universe, the most humungous tower that people have ever built would be as significant as an invisible structure on a microscopic speck of matter 1/100th the size of a grain of sand floating in an ocean. Given what the Bible tells us about the power and majesty of the creator of the universe, is there any way God would feel threatened by a tower of this magnitude?

The Tower of Babel story is clearly a work of fiction. Unfortunately, in Western culture we have taken on a very cramped view of what fiction is and can do. In presentations during author visits, when I was younger and meaner than I am today, I used to ask people what's the difference between fiction and nonfiction? I could always get this answer: *nonfiction is something that is true and fiction is something that is not true.* Wrong!

"Have you read *Mein Kampf* by Adolph Hitler?" I would ask. "That's nonfiction. You're telling me what he wrote is true?" I don't think so. On the other hand, there are many works of fiction that have touched my heart with the truth in a way that no factual reporting could. I suspect they understood stories in biblical times better than we obsessive fact-crunchers and reality TV-watchers of today. When David committed his sin with Bathsheba in 2 Samuel, the way the prophet Nathan got David to recognize the truth was to tell him a story that is pure fiction. Truth came to David through fiction. Good fiction is not only true, it lays bare truths that we could see in no other way.

I can illustrate the truth-telling power of story through my own experience. I used to do a lot of traveling and speaking in schools because I could make more money talking about what I had written than I did from writing it. There were only two times in all my travels when I ran into discipline problems, where the behavior situation was spinning out of control and school authorities were doing nothing about it.

In those situations, I stopped my presentation and began to tell a story. The setting was Minneapolis, shortly after I was born. The Minneapolis Symphony agreed to put on a special performance for area school children. When the day arrived, buses came from all over the Metro area to facilitate this event. Every seat in the Minneapolis Auditorium was filled. The lights dimmed, and the conductor walked out onto the stage. As he reached center stage and bowed to the applauding audience, some kid yelled out: "Nice tux, Freddie!" The conductor stared in icy silence at the audience, then turned and walked off the stage. That was the end of the performance. Several thousand students had to go home without hearing a single note played. All the expense for dozens of school districts, of buses and drivers, all the logistics of transporting students, an entire school day—all wasted because one kid did not know how to act. Because one kid thought he was clever.

After telling that to my audience, I stared icily at them and asked a simple question. "Do you know why I'm telling you that story?" The silence and tension that fell over the room gave me their answer. They knew very well why I told the story. It was a warning, and it had its intended effect.

Is that story of the symphony conductor historically accurate? I doubt it. I heard the story only once, from a teacher, back when I was in fifth grade. I have never talked to anyone who can corroborate the story; never found a shred of supporting evidence that it ever happened. If I had to guess, I would say it is based on a factual event, but my version of it cannot be factually accurate. Trying to construct accurate details of a story I heard third-hand 35 years ago is impossible.

But historical precision was not the point of the story. I was not telling it so that students would have at their disposal the facts of a verifiable incident. I was telling it because it was the best way to drive home a truth that they could not seem to grasp in any other way: The truth that I was not there to babysit them. The truth that even though I had traveled a long way and people had gone to some effort and cost to get me there, I was this close to walking out of the room, and they would have had to live with the consequences of their actions.

So when I read the story of the tower of Babel I hear the voice of God asking, "Do you know why I'm telling you this story?"

Because it's full of historical facts that we somehow need to know? Or because it tells us a truth about God and ourselves in an especially insightful way? The point of the story has to do with pride. The people of Babel thought they were hot stuff. They were so impressed with themselves that they believed they were as good as God, maybe better. They could run the world without regard for anything or anyone else.

According to the story, what does that attitude lead to? Chaos. It's the old principle that pride goes before a fall. When people do not understand their place in the scheme of life and do not acknowledge the presence of an all-encompassing, cohesive force in the universe, everything breaks down. When we put ourselves at the center of the universe, we can no longer relate to one another. We cannot speak to each other in any meaningful way. When it's every person for himself or herself, we go our separate ways; when we look after only our own interests, we scatter across the face of the earth.

I suppose Genesis could have said it just the way I did. But the story of the Tower of Babel was a much more compelling and effective way of getting that point across. So is this just an old tale with no relevance for today? I think it's more timely now than when it was written. Human arrogance has never been greater. With every scientific advancement in technology and genetic engineering, we get a higher opinion of ourselves. Look what we can do! We can harness the power of the atom; we can cram billions of bits of information onto a chip the size of a pin head. We can manipulate the building blocks of nature to clone and create new forms of life. We can arrest the aging process and defeat disease. We can build a skyscraper 2700 feet high.

We are such hot stuff! We can utterly dominate the natural world and everything in it. We are our own god. We don't need any other.

The story of the tower of Babel reminds us that in the grand scheme of existence, every human achievement of which we boast is as significant as an invisible structure on a microscopic bit of matter attached to a grain of sand suspended in the ocean. It warns us that when we stake our claim as the masters of creation, we are setting ourselves up for a gigantic fall. In the language of the universe, prideful boasts are nothing but incoherent babble. They cause us to lose our ability to connect with the world, with each other. Our chances of accomplishing anything real and lasting, anything approaching the glorious new kingdom of God, disintegrate. We fall into chaos.

Contrast that with the story of Pentecost in Acts. This story has more of a historical, eyewitness quality about it that puts it in the nonfiction genre. But as with all stories, the important thing to ask is "Why is God telling us this story?"

Pentecost begins exactly where Babel ends. It begins in chaos. The disciples are confused and uncertain of their place in the world. Jerusalem is filled with people from all over the world, each speaking their own language, unable to communicate with each other, to connect with each other. This is a world struggling to find hope, direction, and meaning. Unlike the people of Babel, the disciples do not fall into the trap of pride. They do not assume they are the masters of all they survey, answerable to none. They acknowledge God as the source of life, and recognize that whatever they can achieve in life flows from the gifts of their loving creator. They understand that their role in the world is not to pump themselves up by building towers over the bodies of anyone who gets in their way, but to build peace that lifts up the souls of all in need. What they are in desperate need of is some guidance for taking on this mission.

Like the people of Babel, the disciples begin speaking in tongues. But when they do so, it has the opposite effect. They do not speak in some strange babble that no one can understand, but rather in recognizable languages that proclaim and make known the power of the Gospel. Speaking in tongues in the Babel story divided and scattered the people. Speaking in tongues at

Pentecost drew the people together.

When we try to build monuments to ourselves, when we think that equality with God is a thing to be grasped, we fall into chaos. We become divided and scattered. We cannot speak with each other; we cannot connect with each other. Like a certain Iraqi dictator who tried to make himself into a god, we end up face down in the dirt with broken bits of our monument lying around us.

For the Christian, there is one who can turn babble into coherence, chaos into order, division into unity. Someone who can reforge our connections with each other and with creation. That person is a carpenter from Nazareth who, as Philippians says, though he was in the form of God, did not count equality with God a thing to be grasped, but emptied himself, taking the form of a servant. Over 2000 years later, his spirit continues to speak the language of healing and peace that brings together people of all nations. When we speak in his name, we speak in a language that is different from our native tongue. We speak in that universal language that is understood by all and draws us all together.

That is the only kind of speaking in tongues with which I am familiar, and it is truly a gift of the Spirit.

Part IV

Questions about Creation

Chapter 15

I Wonder:
Can the universe exist without God?

A long time ago I was introduced to a concept called "the God of the gaps." This philosophy says that religion exists to offer explanations to those questions that cannot currently be explained. As science uncovers more and more explanations for reality that contradict religious explanations, the relevance and credibility of religion shrinks. For example, the medieval religious view of the earth at the center of the universe provided an explanation for ordered nature that was accepted until this was disproved by science, against the strenuous and sometimes violent objections of religious authorities.

There is some obvious truth in the premise of God of the gaps. But, taken to the extreme, this point of view argues that religion will become obsolete as scientific discovery eventually fills in all of our gaps in knowledge.

As a microbiologist/pastor, I find most turf wars between science and religion to be pointless. The Bible does not help me at all in understanding auto mechanics, photosynthesis, or geology. I need science for that. Science is of no use to me in understanding what I am to do with the life I have been given or how I am to relate to those with whom I share the earth. I rely on theological exploration for that.

My inclination, then, is to turn the tables on the God of the gaps mentality. Rather than focusing on religious overreach into scientific reality, I wonder what would happen if we focused on the areas in which religious teaching contributes more than science to a more accurate understanding of the world we live in. The subject of creation is a place where those boundaries between religion and science get fuzzy. It is especially important when reading Genesis and discussing religious doctrine to recognize when we are asking scientific questions and when we are asking religious questions, and so that would be a good place to start.

My wonderings about the God of the gaps have taken me on a wild ride through the universe in search of God. It's a long-distance trip and in order to get where we want to go, we'll have to ride on the wings of science for a way. We must let science take us as far as it can, and when it is no longer useful, see if the Bible can carry us from there.

Scientific inquiry can take us all the way back to the second verse of the Bible. We read in Genesis 1 that, prior to creation, the universe was without form and void. Genesis and science both bring us back to the point at which nothing was there. Creation is the event that put something there. The question of *what* happened at creation is a question for science, not religion. You're just not going to get good answers to scientific questions from writers who believed the earth was flat and that there was a partition called the firmament that separated earth from the heavens. Science has tools for getting answers about the physical reality of the earth; religion does not.

As near as we can figure, this thing called the universe came into being about 15 billion years ago, with a fantastic explosion of matter. Why do scientists believe that? The simplified explanation is that if you trace the paths of all the large objects in the sky and work backwards along the same trajectories, everything ends up starting in the same place.

In asking the question of what happened at creation, however, we have reached the limit of where science can take us. Where was God in the creation of the universe, and what difference would it make if God were not there at all? That is where theology has to take over.

The question of where God was at creation brings up a puzzling question about time. Did time come into existence with the creation of the universe? If so, that implies that there was a point at which time did not exist, followed by a point at which time did exist. If that is true, then at some point, time was created.

How did that happen? How was time created? That is really a more interesting question than how was the universe created, and it is not something science can answer. On the other hand, if time did not come into existence with creation, then time must have already existed before creation. If time existed before creation, then creation does not take us back to the beginning at all. We have to go back further than creation and again, that takes us into a place where science is not equipped to go. So, it is left to us in the religious field to try and provide an explanation for time from outside the realm of science.

Genesis is a good place to look. It has a profound comment on this situation couched within the first of its creation stories. Notice that Genesis 1 does not say, "In the beginning, creation." It says, "In the beginning, God." The world did not start with creation. The world started with God. Which is exactly the point of that long creation story.

Therein lies a way of solving the problem of time. God is not bound by time. Christians say this in our creeds and in our faith statements when we speak about life everlasting. With God, you never reach a point at which time ends. With God, time stretches on to infinity in eternal life. If God is not bound by time in the future, then it works the same way in the reverse direction, in the past. There is no point in the future at which God ends and there is no point in the past at which God begins.

Whether time existed before creation or whether it began at creation is not something anyone can answer, and really, it does not matter. With God, there is no unaccounted-for emptiness lying there before time came into being. With God, there is no unaccounted-for emptiness if time existed before creation. Either way, God was already there.

This leads to a second issue: the creation of something from nothing. Science deals with systems and laws and cause-and-effect. There is nothing in science that can explain the creation of something out of nothing.

How can time not exist, and then suddenly exist? Where did the components of the matter that blew into existence at the beginning of creation come from? At some point in any discussion of creation, you run into a huge wall with the transition between when nothing existed and when something existed. How do you get something out of nothing?

No matter how hard I search, God is the only answer I can find to the question of how do you get something from nothing. With a reversely infinite God, there never was a time when there was nothing.

Psalm 89 speculates that there was a time when north and south did not exist. Then suddenly they existed. But they did not come from nothing because something was there. God was there. Genesis provides an explanation to the scientific dilemma of something being created out of nothing. The universe was created out of something. It was created out of God. Again, that was the point of the creation story. The details, which were God-of-the-gaps guesswork, are not the issue. The point is the universe was created because God made it happen. Christians declare that to be true. If we are smart, we leave it to science to explore *how* that universe came into being and has developed into what it is today.

Another question that only theology can answer is: what difference would it make if God did not exist? In trying to imagine a universe without God, we have to admit, first of all, that it just might be an impossible task. We do not know of any other way to explain how something comes from nothing. We cannot explain how the universe, what we know as reality, **could** exist if not for God.

That means that the question of what would the universe be like without God has a very simple answer. If you could erase every thought from your head, every feeling, every sensation, that's what the universe would be like without God. It would be, as Genesis says, without form and void.

Since a viable universe does not appear to be possible in the absence of God, we'll have to change our question: Instead of asking what the universe would be like without God, let's narrow the focus by asking what would the universe be like if God were not exactly the God revealed to us in the Bible? The God revealed in the Bible has four main characteristics:

Power
Faithfulness
Love
Wisdom

Let's review some of what we have covered in previous chapters to imagine a universe ruled by a God *without* those traits:

Power

I have had the privilege of camping in the Minnesota Boundary Waters, a place where motorized transportation is not allowed. Planes are not allowed to fly over it. The crystal-clear sky is so thick with stars you cannot begin to count them. Each of those stars is enormous and distant to a degree we cannot comprehend. As I sat watching these stars, I was blown away by the fact that some of the light I was seeing started its journey to earth hundreds of millions of years ago, long before the dinosaurs roamed the earth. I was seeing an image that, traveling at 177,000 miles/per second, took that long to reach us. The size and scope of this universe makes our lives ridiculously puny.

I submit to you that only a God powerful beyond our understanding could create such a universe and exert the kind of control over it that has made life possible. Were God not as powerful as the Bible claims, any attempt to create a universe would produce, at best, a chaotic wasteland — without form and void.

Faithfulness

Our universe is governed by laws: of gravity, thermodynamics, electromagnetism, chemistry and is, to a large degree, predictable. It has patterns, seasons, continuity. It runs on order and logic. We can understand so much of our world because we can count on it being, in most ways, the same today as it was yesterday. The earth will orbit the sun in a predictable way—it will not randomly spin free of the sun's gravitational pull. Chemical reactions will occur faithfully, providing food and oxygen, our senses will give us generally accurate and reliable information about our surroundings. That could happen only in a universe in which God is faithful.

We can count on God to be who God is. We can count on God's universe to be what God made it to be. If God were not as faithful as the Bible claims, we would live in a baffling, magical world. That may sound like fun and sheer fantasy. But imagine living in a world where things happen for no reason, where the only way anything ever survives is by sheer luck. A universe in which God is not faithful would be a nightmare of insanity.

Love

Imagine if everything in the universe were 100% reliable and predictable. Imagine a world in which everything happens according to a plan, a formula. It would be very easy on God. It would be easy on us. No problems, ever. Religious people with a "control freak" view of God believe this to be the case. But if the universe were like that, nothing new would ever take place. Imagine a universe in which choices do not exist. Where life simply repeats itself in an endless cycle. Nothing ever changes or evolves. I don't think you could call that life at all.

It would be a robotic world, a sterile world of machines, performing exactly as engineered. It would be a crushingly dull universe in which nothing surprising, interesting, or important would ever happen.

A world without love would be a world that existed only for the creator, shared with no one—devoid of any meaning.

Wisdom

How do you create a universe that balances the opposite needs of faithfulness and love? That preserves enough order so that we can understand and depend upon it, yet creates enough change and spontaneity and chance and surprise and choice so that what we know as life can exist? It takes incredible wisdom to figure out how to keep those in balance.

Genetics may provide some insight into how God reconciles opposites to achieve that balance: How does God demonstrate faithfulness, preserving order and dependability in reproduction, i.e. the creation of new life? Through the use of DNA replication, a template system that makes offspring in the image of their parents. This process transfers thousands of traits from one generation to the next so that there is continuity. So that baby humans do not come out as ostriches, or bacteria, or cabbages but as something very much like what the parents were. At the same time, God uses random genetic recombination, jumping genes, and mutation so that at each birth a new person is created, a person entirely different from any that ever existed before. Possibility and change have been built into the system.

If God were not wise, the delicate balances of nature required to keep such diametrically opposed concepts as faithfulness and love in balance would be impossible to achieve. All life would be lurching between twin extremes of chaos and meaningless mechanical existence.

Agnostics point to the intricate systems and laws of nature and say that these are what run the world, not God. But there is nothing scientific in such proclamations. In science, you do not get something from nothing. Processes do not create themselves; laws do not create themselves.

Power does not just happen.

Faithfulness does not just happen.

Love does not just happen.

Wisdom does not just happen.

The fact that the universe exists as it does can be explained by the words of Genesis: "In the beginning, God." The universe works because of God, who is powerful, faithful, loving, and wise.

The wisdom of God determined that what makes existence most worthwhile is relationship. So, God created us and the universe to share relationship. Relationship cannot happen between strangers. That means we cannot share any relationship with God if we do not know God. Yet an infinite God is so far beyond us. As Darwin said when asked his view of God, "A dog might as well speculate on the mind of (Isaac) Newton."

We cannot know anything about God unless God chooses to make it known—unless God chooses to come to us and reveal it in a way we can understand. That would explain the purpose and nature of Scripture. Those writings declare that the first step in God coming to us was the creation of a huge and complex universe built on faithfulness, love, and wisdom to reflect what God is, so that we would know who God is. And that was only the start. God kept finding more and better ways to come to us, to reveal more and more to us about who God is. Christians believe that the best of those ways was the sending of Jesus, who is called Immanuel, or "God with us."

I can understand God best by looking around and wondering at the cosmos. From the tiniest particle of matter to the vastness of the greatest galaxy, God is there. The whole universe declares what the Bible declares, that God has come in power, in wisdom, in faithfulness, and in love to share with us the gift of life.

Chapter 16

I Wonder:
How can you reconcile the theory of evolution with the book of Genesis?

As we discussed earlier, the Christian church, centuries ago made it a matter of doctrine that the sun revolves around the earth. After all, according to the church, that's what the Bible said. You had to believe that to be a Christian in good standing. You could not question it. If, like Galileo and Copernicus, you questioned this "truth," the church authorities threatened you with torture, death, and eternal damnation.

The evidence that the earth revolves around the sun eventually grew so overwhelming that no one questions it today. Frankly, it made the church look pretty stupid. I have often wondered how many thousands of people were driven away from any chance of hearing the Christian message by this stubborn misreading of the truth by pious Christians. When those who claim to offer the Absolute Truth are proven wrong on a key point of their argument, they lose all credibility. The church put a huge obstacle in the way of educated people accepting the Christian message.

Today, the same mistake is being made. Churches with a literal view of the Bible insist that Christians must believe in creationism, not evolution. As they do so, the numbers of unchurched climb steadily, even as research shows the hunger for spirituality in our society is growing. Is there a connection? I can't prove anything. But I do know that this view of creationism has given people a strong reason to reject the whole Christian message.

Our young people, especially, are wondering about this. Requiring blind obedience to irrational ideas is never a good idea in this world. It's how cults get started. If young people cannot square what the church says with what they understand to be true about the world, it does not matter what or how you teach: they will not look to Christianity for answers. That is why I believe it is crucial to the faith that we speak up on this issue.

My ponderings of this issue have led me to believe that evolution makes far more sense than creationism, not only from a scientific standpoint, but from both a biblical and theological standpoint as well. It may surprise some that I base support of evolution on the Bible as much as science. The key question I hear is, "If evolution is true, why would God allow a mistaken account to begin the Bible, the inspired Word of God?"

I don't believe Genesis is mistaken. I believe it is misunderstood, in two ways: The first misunderstanding is about context—the knowledge of the time. What does the Genesis creation account say about the laws of thermodynamics? How about gravity? Do any of the Psalms deal with lasers or cell phones or electricity? Did Jesus tell any parables about NFL playoff teams or nuclear warheads? Of course not. When the Bible was written, these things were unknown. Had Genesis spoken of them, no one would have known what they were talking about. It would have been a jumble of fantasy of no use to anyone, and so never would have been preserved. Similarly, if it spoke of organic chemicals and a swirling cosmic soup and evolution, it would have made no sense to anyone. First rule of evangelism: The Word of God always comes to people in the context in which they live.

So let's look at the context in the time of Genesis:

Chapter 1:6 *And God said, "Let there be a dome in the midst of the waters, and let it separate the waters from the waters." So God made the dome and separated the waters that were under the dome from the waters above it. And God called the dome "sky."*

Those verses give a clear idea of the context of the times. In the prevailing world view, the earth was flat, and the sky was a solid structure that separated the earth from the water surrounding it. Rain occurred when that water leaked through the dome. Genesis cannot help but speak to the context in which it was written. The question is, does anyone live in that context today?

1:3–4 *Then God said, "Let there be light," and there was light. And God saw that the light was good; and God separated the light from the darkness. God called the light Day, and the darkness he called Night. And there was evening and there was morning, the first day.*

DAY ONE: 1:14 *God said, "Let there be lights in the dome of the sky." God made the two great lights—the greater light to rule the day and the lesser light to rule the night. God set them in the dome of the sky to give light upon the earth.*

DAY FOUR: According to the sequence provided here, God created light on day one and then created day and night, evening and morning, but did not create the sun until day four. Although I can't follow their logic, apparently that worked in their understanding of the cosmos. It does not work in ours. By definition, you cannot have day and night on this earth without sun.

Today, any science textbook more than 20 years old is so outdated as to be virtually useless. It no longer reflects the understood reality of our context. Does it make any sense to be using a 2500-year-old book as a science text?

Even more important than context is purpose. Genesis could not have been intended as a science text because science did not exist. I have enormous respect for the Bible as the inspired Word of God. Respect means paying serious attention to what I am reading. The Bible is not God's personal diary dictated to stenographers. It is not even a book. It is a library of books that includes history, poetry, letters, advice, proclamation, parables, hymns, fiction, and legal codes.

So what kind of a book is Genesis?

Chapter 1:11 *Then God said, "Let the earth put forth vegetation, plants, and fruit trees." And there was evening and morning: the **third day**.*

Move on to the **sixth** day: 1:24 *God made the animals—everything that crawls upon the earth.* 1:26 *Then God said, "Let us make humankind in our own image."* The order is clear: plants, animals, humans. Now go to 2:4: *In the day that the Lord God made the earth and the heavens, when no plant of the field was yet in the earth, then the Lord God formed man from the dust of the ground.* 2:18 *Then the Lord God said, "It is not good that man should be alone. So out of the ground the Lord God formed every animal of the field."* What's the order here? Clearly: humans first, then plants and animals.

So if the Genesis creation story is to be taken as literal fact, we have a problem. There is not one creation story. There are two, and the facts do not agree. If you talk about the Bible only in literal terms, then if one is correct, the other is mistaken.

What happened? Were the writers of Genesis so stupid or careless that they did not notice such a glaring contradiction? I don't think so. It makes more sense that the writers of Genesis, inspired by God, knew exactly what they were doing. They were not called to create a science text. They were called to proclaim the truth in their own time and place about who created the world and what kind of being that creator is. The details of the story were not the focus. The focus was on providing an introduction to the Bible by telling two stories from their tradition that, taken together, lay out clearly and simply what the entire Bible is about.

The first creation story (Genesis 1) proclaims God as the awesome creator of the universe, a being powerful beyond comprehension—the one who somehow brought into being everything that exists in our universe.

The second creation story (Genesis 2) brings to the world the astounding claim that, despite being majestic beyond comprehension, this creator is interested in us. Genesis 2 argues that this awesome creative force that we met in Chapter One brought us into existence out of love and a compulsion to share that love.

The overwhelming majority of experts in the fields of biology and earth science accept that the earth and its species have evolved over time. Their arguments are so compelling to the peer review system as to be established science. So instead of denying the obvious and making science the enemy, I suggest we listen to what scientists have to say. Genesis describes a God as powerful as the limit of the writers' imaginations could conceive. Science has merely expanded the limit of our imagination. Thanks to science, we now know a lot more than did the writers of Genesis about how powerful God is.

They had no clue just how large a territory God roams. To review once again, they didn't know that there are more stars in the universe than can be counted, or that the number of light years to the edge of the visible universe is 1 followed by 24 zeros. And that's just the part that we can see.

In fact, the more scientific evidence we get, the more clearly we see the hand of the Creator in the world. Have you ever wondered why there are trillions and trillions of stars? Does it seem like a huge waste, or proof that we are utterly insignificant? It's neither. John Polkinghorne argues that the universe had to be that big in order to create us. Only a cosmos this enormous could last for the 15 billion years required to evolve life as we know it: 10 billion to create carbon and the other necessary elements, 5 billion to shape that into human life.

If you look at the history of biological evolution, so many things had to happen just when they did in order to produce us. Climatic changes, disappearance of dinosaurs. If you reran the history of the earth a billion times, the odds are you would never again end up with anything approaching human life.

What explains the fact that the only universe we know of happened to have literally thousands of the exact trillion-to-one events occur in the exact order required to create the conscious life form known as us? The only explanation that makes rational sense is that some incredibly powerful being directed the whole show with the object of producing us. And where have we heard that before? That is exactly the story that Genesis tells.

For me, one of the strongest arguments in favor of evolution is a theological one. Creationism says that God created the world all at once long ago and that it has remained static. Do you know any creative people? Creative people love to create. They *must* create. There isn't one of them I have ever met who would create something and then say, "There, I'm done creating for the rest of my life." Does it make any sense that God, the most creative force in the universe, had one fit of creative activity and never had the urge to create anything again?

Listen to the Bible's third creation story, from the Gospel of John. "All things came into being through him, and without him not one thing came into being. What has come into being in him was LIFE." Life is not a sterile universe where nothing is ever new, nothing new is created. Life grows and changes, and evolves into new life.

God is not just the person who created the world. God is the person who created the world and has been creating it ever since, and is still creating it today, and will continue to create it long after we are gone.

Genesis basically says two profound things: 1) The God who created all this is awesome beyond our imagination. 2) That incredibly powerful being loves you, with a love that is equally unimaginable.

That is the Bible in a nutshell. The rest is just details.

Part V

Questions about Prayer

Chapter 17

I Wonder:
Everyone who has ever been prayed for is either dead or will die. How then does faith heal?

Mark's Gospel weaves together the stories of two desperate people who turn to Jesus for healing. The one that has had more influence concerning faith healing is the woman who suffered from hemorrhages for 12 years.

This unnamed woman has tried everything. In a way that echoes today's health care reality, her search for a cure has drained her of all her resources. She has seen every physician she could find, tried every treatment imaginable. She has left no stone unturned in her search for healing. Nothing has worked. In fact, she has only been getting worse. Yet she refuses to give up. She keeps searching for any possible cure. The latest folk remedy she has heard is Jesus. Word on the street is that Jesus is healing people of whatever ails them. *Let's give it a try.*

She finds out where Jesus is traveling and hurries to him, only to find him mobbed by a huge crowd, all there for the same thing, all clamoring for Jesus' attention. She decides that all she needs to do is touch Jesus' cloak and she will be healed. The story does not say how she came to this conclusion. Maybe the crowd was so huge she thought Jesus could not possibly get around to her. Maybe she thought Jesus charged a fee for his cures: she has no money, so she's going to try to sneak a cure without anyone knowing so she doesn't have to pay.

Whatever, she squeezes through the crowd behind him and touches his cloak. Immediately she feels that she is healed of her disease. Her plan worked! Only she doesn't get away with it. Jesus senses her presence, turns around and says, "Who touched my cloak?"

To the disciples, it was a ridiculous question. As they were milling through the crowd, dozens, if not hundreds of people have brushed against him. They might well have thought a better question would be "Who did *not* touch his cloak?"

But the words pierce the woman's conscience. Instead of melting away into the crowd and enjoying her miraculous, long-sought recovery, she falls down before Jesus and confesses that she tried to sneak a cure from Jesus.

Having done so, she dreads the punishment that will follow from having tried to cheat such a powerful man. At the least, she expects he will rescind her fraudulently obtained cure and all her hopes will be dashed again.

Instead, Jesus looks at her with what seems to be admiration. "Daughter, your faith has made you well," he says. "Go in peace and be healed of your disease." *Your faith has made you well.*

So many desperate people have latched on to this story and to those words in times of illness or tragedy. Like this woman, we will try almost anything to be made well. The more desperate we are, the more willing we are to grasp at any straw. Jesus' statement hints at a simple solution. It seems all we need to do is believe that if we can get close enough to Jesus, he will cure us of our ills.

This was the feeling in the Middle Ages, when it was commonly believed that kings were God's anointed leaders on earth and that Jesus' powers of healing had been transferred to them. In the midst of unimaginable suffering and death from the Black Death and other pandemics, word spread that a cure could be found in the touch of the king. The key to healing was to believe this and then get close enough to the king to get his magic touch.

This thinking has infiltrated our civilization in many ways. While vacationing in Lunenburg, Nova Scotia, we learned how dangerous it was to fish in the North Atlantic for a living. Lunenburg, which never had a population larger than 4000, lost upwards of 700 hundred men at sea in the past century. A large stone monument at the wharf lists those locals known to have died on the ships. Whole slabs of this monument are devoted to the dozens upon dozens who perished during the August storms of 1926 and 1927. In the village of Blue Rocks, just outside Lunenburg, the oldest surviving male in 1927 was 13 years of age.

Amid such danger and loss, desperate people searched for something that would protect them. They were willing to try anything in hopes of finding that magic cloak that would keep them safe and well. We listened to a guide describe for more than a half hour the many superstitions that sailors followed, and were told he had barely scratched the surface.

For example, nothing was ever to be turned upside down. Baked bread was to be lifted out of the pan—you never turned over the pan. Turning something upside down meant that a ship was going to flip over. Once a sailor said goodbye to his family at the house to go to the ship, none of them were to speak to him again until his return. If he forgot something he needed, the wife must come up to him from behind and slip the object under his arm, without a word. If a sailor met a priest on the way to the ship, he had to turn around, go back home, and start his trip to the wharf all over again.

Many of these superstitions were religious-based. Sailors were forbidden to say the word, "Pig." They spelled out the word, or referred to these animals as "ground rooters" or "little fellas," but never "pig." Why? Because pigs have cloven feet and supposedly, so does the devil. The devil's name was not to be invoked for any reason.

There was a host of other superstitions designed to ward off evil. An elaborate set of rules was founded on the premise that health and safety could be obtained by faith, by believing in the powers of protection in these rituals, by touching these magic cloaks. Many of us are no different when it comes to searching for the magic cloak that will make us well. We try the latest medical claims, diets, the latest folk cures, and self-help keys to health and happiness. Like the woman in the story, we spend fortunes searching for the secret of wellness. This includes so many desperate people who have come to think that if your faith makes you well, then all you need to be cured of disease and healed of injury is to believe strongly enough. If the cure fails to work, it's only because you don't have enough faith or are not praying hard enough.

Such an interpretation of the story of the hemorrhaging woman has turned many a tragedy into a devastating catastrophe. It has caused those who experience debilitating illness or loss to suffer not only the effects of these hardships but add a heaping dose of either a) **guilt** because their faith was not great enough to save themselves or a loved one or b) **utter rejection** of Christianity because it proved to be a lie.

We saw a haunting example of this while on a walking tour at night in Lunenburg. Our guide took us to a cemetery and shined her light on an old gravestone on which was etched the names of several children from one family. All had died in a short period of time, almost certainly from an epidemic of an infectious disease.

There was also an engraving of a hand holding a scepter, pointing at the ground. Our guide noted that it was common at the time to embellish the gravestone with a picture of a scepter, or some other object pointing to the sky, heavenward—a symbol of hope and faith in God. This downward-pointing scepter was a grim statement that this family had abandoned their faith. They had trusted in faith and prayer and devotion and good works to be the magic cloak that protected them from evil, only to see in the horrible tragedy that had befallen them this was not the case. The family buried their children under this bitter message and left town, never to be heard from again.

What happened? Why didn't it work for them the way it did for the woman whose faith had made her well? Was it their fault;

did they do something wrong? Was their faith too weak? I have often wondered about faith healing or prayers healing. Why do some of the most devout, wonderful Christians suffer and die of terrible diseases while other folks make startling recoveries?

The tragic case of the Lunenburg family highlighted for me three crucial mistakes that have been made in the popular interpretation of the woman whose faith has made her well. First, it ignores the other healing story with which it is sandwiched. This is the story of a synagogue leader named Jairus, whose daughter lies deathly ill. Jairus is so desperate to save his daughter that he dares go against his peers who dislike and distrust Jesus. He comes to Jesus and asks for help in healing his daughter.

But it turns out that he is too late. Word comes to him that the girl has died before Jesus can get there. When Jesus insists that the child may yet be healed, what response does he get? A powerful profession of faith in the one who can do all things? No, verse 40 says, "They laughed at him." Whatever faith they had in Jesus is gone. They are openly scornful of Jesus' power to affect the situation. They are ready to put the child in the ground and erect the hand with the scepter pointing down.

What happens then in this situation where there is no faith? The girl is healed. Wait a minute, how did that happen? Wasn't it faith that made the bleeding woman well? Yet Jesus healed the little girl despite the complete lack of faith of those who cared for her. I don't think it is an accident that these two incidents are interwoven in the Gospel. One story seems to balance the other.

Faith is not the catalyst that causes God to cure the illness. When Jesus said, "Your faith has made you well," he was telling the truth that faith brings about good results. But the other story, where healing occurs without faith, in the face of open ridicule, demonstrates that faith is not necessary to bring about physical healing.

A second factor in these stories is that this woman did not have what we would call devout faith. Jesus was not her first choice, or second, or third. She tried a hundred cures before she turned to him. I would imagine she approached each one of her previous cures with the same passionate faith she brought to Jesus. She was desperate; she would try anything. If you told her that rubbing the head of a blue salamander would cure her; she would have rushed out to find a blue salamander with all the haste that she set out to see Jesus, and would trust in that cure just as strongly as she trusted in Jesus.

Is hoping that Jesus could do something for her a sign of a Christian faith so strong as to produce miracles? If that were the case, her actions would have set off a stampede of sick and injured people rushing to touch Jesus. I don't think Jesus wanted that. I don't think he was saying that her brazenness in touching his cloak made her well.

Third, Jesus said to the woman, "Your faith has made you well." He did not say, "your faith has made you immortal." Every sick or hurt person who has ever been prayed for in this world is either dead or will die. The point of the story cannot be that faith in Jesus protects you from harm or will cure anything that strikes. The key is what Jesus says directly after saying "Your faith has made you well." He says, "Go in peace."

Think back a moment to the tragic family at the cemetery who had lost their faith. I have no reason to criticize them. I cannot imagine being in their shoes, nor can I pretend to know how I would have reacted. But I have a good idea of how that loss of faith affected their wellness. How meaningful and productive do you think the rest of their lives were? How generous, how joyful, how vibrant? Without faith, they had no particular reason to live, nothing for which to hope. In rejecting God, it is hard to imagine they experienced any peace, any healing in their lives.

When Jesus said to the woman, "Your faith has made you well," I suspect Jesus was commending her faith in life, that in spite of years of failure, she refused to give up hope. I think he praised her for clinging to her faith, in the face of tremendous odds and evidence to the contrary, that tomorrow was going to be worth living, that God had something more to give her. *But for her faith that there was a reason to keep living in the face of tragedy, she would not have been there for Jesus to heal her.*

Jesus commended the woman for her faith in basic goodness, honesty, in right and wrong. For standing up and admitting what she had done in touching his cloak, when she could so easily have gotten away with it. For having such strong faith in God's eternal justice that she refused to fight evil with evil, to let desperation trump decency. Because she had that faith, she could be at peace with herself, with her world and with her God. Jesus saw that whatever storms of life battered her, she would weather them; she would be healed.

Faith is not access to a magic cloak that will cure all illness. But our faith *does* make us well. I have seen this in funeral homes in my ministry. Death is difficult for everyone, whether they have faith or not. Any deep loss sickens the soul and robs us of peace, regardless of our faith or lack of it. The difference I have seen that faith makes is this. People who have no active faith, no hope of eternal life, no connection with a living God or a community of believers, so often have nowhere to turn, no solid ground upon which to stand in times of death. They have nothing to protect them against bitterness and confusion. There is no healing for them, except for the passage of time, which works like novocaine to deaden the nerves so that they can no longer feel the emptiness that is there.

People of faith tend to experience healing. They may carry deep scars, all of their lives, but they experience healing. Enough so they can go on, rebuild their lives, rediscover joy and meaning in life, and see a future that is better, where God will wipe away every tear, and pain and sorrow will be no more.

What I get from these stories is that faith will not bring you riches or good fortune. It will not heal your every illness. Your faith will not prevent death, pain, or sorrow, although there will be times when you are spared these things. Your faith *will* make you well; so that you can go in peace and be healed. That is what faith can do. If faith does not do that, then your faith is misplaced. If faith raises false hopes and unrealistic expectations, then your faith is not a strength but a burden that will drag you down into the pit of disillusionment and despair.

If faith does not bring life, healing and peace to you and those around you, then I don't care what you believe or how strongly you believe it—your faith is no good to you or anyone else.

Jesus came to bring life into the world; that you may know the joy of being connected in relationship to God and creation. Faith in that will make you well. *Go in peace and be healed.*

Chapter 18

I Wonder:
What does it mean to "call upon the Lord?" What kind of calls does God accept?

On a camping trip a few years ago, we took time to visit the Villa Louis, the restored Prairie du Chien home of Wisconsin's first millionaire. Our guide described the process of a social visit back in the nineteenth century, at least at this level of society.

After you were let off at the gate, you would walk up the tree-lined front walk to the porch, and ring the doorbell. When one of the servants answered, you would present a card with your name printed on it. It did not matter whether you were a best friend or neighbor or a salesman; you had to show your card. The servant would then invite you in to a comfortable hallway, and go off to deliver your calling card. You would sit in the waiting area until such time as the person you had come to visit could see you.

A social visit was not a spur of the moment thing, done on a whim. You had to reserve a significant block of time, you had to follow a particular set of rules, and the entire process was controlled by the person you wanted to visit.

Thanks to cell phones and texting, the concept of visiting has entirely changed. We can contact anyone at any time in any place. We can enter a person's home from halfway around the world, while we're pulling into a parking lot, exercising on a trail, or doing the dishes. We can text someone in the middle of a sermon.

A similar thing has happened with trade or commerce. A Pakistani professor explained to me the tradition of bartering in many nations around the world. It exists not, as I had believed, to turn every transaction into a stressful, cutthroat competition that tests a person's negotiating skills, but because it facilitates human interaction. An exchange of goods between two persons is considered an honored and important event. It is always personal. The barter system provides time and a framework for personal interaction.

The professor pointed out how bewildered his family were by the modern American supermarket, where hundreds of dollars of goods are transferred from one person to another with scarcely any eye contact. Where the only human interaction is "Did you find what you needed?" "That'll be $69.45, please," and "have a nice day."

They find stock market exchanges even more baffling, where billions of dollars of assets change hands without any party in the transfer even knowing that the other party exists. And don't even try to explain phone transactions that take place without ever getting an actual human voice on the other end.

I wonder about this dynamic when I think of the subject of prayer. What does it mean to call upon the name of the Lord? How do you connect with God? Does it mean firing off an instant message, or does it mean going through an elaborate formal ritual? Does it mean communicating quickly and efficiently, or does it mean taking time to enter into some sort of structured personal interaction?

This vital issue lies at the heart of almost every worship conflict in the church. Is worship about easy access to God? What we refer to as contemporary worship leans in this direction. The idea is to eliminate all barriers that lie between the average person and God. Everything is made more accessible and streamlined and informal so that even those with no experience with an organized church can take part and feel comfortable.

Or is worship about establishing a respectful interaction with a God beyond our understanding? What we refer to as traditional worship leans in this direction. The idea is to take the time to learn a protocol that is designed to show respect and honor for God. Everything is more formal and dignified to facilitate an unhurried exploration of the mystery and majesty of God and our relationship with that God.

People tend to lean one way or the other. Those brought up in a more formal, slower-paced world, where respect was paramount, tend to prefer traditional. Those brought up in a faster-paced world, where efficiency is paramount, tend to prefer contemporary. But the issue goes way beyond individual preferences. According to Paul's letter to the Romans, salvation itself is tied up in this matter of calling on the Lord. "Everyone who calls on the name of the Lord shall be saved."

With so much at stake, we need to have a clear idea of what it means to call upon the Lord. Is it primarily a matter of respect or of access, or something in between?

There is a passage from 1 Kings that explores this question. The prophet Elijah is on the run. He has gotten into a war with the prophets who worship Baal, the Canaanite god. Israel's King Ahab and Queen Jezebel have fallen away from the Lord; they, too, are worshippers of Baal. They have put a price on Elijah's head: Wanted, dead or alive. So, Elijah is hiding out. His allegiance to God has gotten him into trouble, and it makes sense to him that God should take some responsibility for getting him out of it. Elijah calls on the Lord to do that. The Lord responds by saying, "Go out and stand on the mountain and let's talk." Elijah does as he is told. Almost immediately, a powerful wind blows through the mountains, so powerful that it shatters rocks. Just what you would hope. Elijah has called on the Lord. He has instant access to God, who has answered immediately, and arrived in this furious storm to rescue the prophet. Except that God was not in the wind.

Puzzled, Elijah waits awhile longer. Here comes an earthquake that shakes the earth and splits the rocks. Surely, God has answered the call this time. The wind was just a preview, and now God has arrived in this even more frightening display of power. Except that God was not in the earthquake.

Elijah's getting a little impatient by now. He called upon

God; God told him that God would be coming. So where is God? Elijah expects an answer to his call.

Then comes a roaring fire that lights up the mountainside, burning everything in its path. Another devastating, frightening event. But it makes sense; God has been showing Elijah the range of his power, the power he will unleash at Elijah's beckoning, because Elijah called on him. Except that God was not in the fire.

After all these furious acts of nature disappear, what happens next is so startling that the Hebrew translators are not quite sure what to make of it. The NIV translation says, "After the fire came a gentle whisper." The NRSV describes it even more dramatically: "After the fire, a sound of sheer silence."

What is clear is that when Elijah calls upon the Lord, God does not come to him in a sudden rush or a violent appearance. Instead, Elijah's call is met by silence and stillness and reflection. This is where Elijah finds the voice of the Lord.

It turns out that access to God is not so easy or simple. You don't just snap your fingers or swipe your credit card and God appears. Calling upon the Lord involves time, it involves listening, and paying attention. It comes through interaction, not easy access.

On the other hand, listen to what happens when Elijah tries to restrict access to God. "I have been very zealous for the Lord," he says, proudly. "The Israelites have rejected your covenant. I am the only one left."

What he is saying is, "It's just you and me, Lord. I am the only one who has been faithful. I am the only one who worships the way it's supposed to be done." The implication is, "Because of my extraordinary faithfulness to you, I expect special access and special treatment."

Listen to God's response to that in his last statement after giving Elijah his instructions: "Yet I reserve 7000 in Israel—all whose knees have not bowed down to Baal."

There's a little pinprick to burst Elisha's bubble of pride. You say you are the only one left. The only one doing it right. The only one who deserves access to me. That is not true; there are thousands just like you.

In other words, when you call on the Lord, leave your pride at home. Do not claim special access to God. Don't expect to leap over others to claim God's attention just because you're so pious. Yes, God is worthy of respect and honor, but God is also open and available to *all* who call upon God's name.

This paradox between respect and access becomes even more striking in the Gospel story of Peter walking on water. Peter sees Jesus coming across the water. He calls upon the Lord, "Lord, if it is you, command me to come to you on the water." This is the epitome of the instant access Christian. Peter acts very familiarly toward Jesus, like they are a couple of fishing buddies. When he calls on Jesus, he tells him what he wants Jesus to do. And it's not anything Peter *needs* to do. It's not anything that would benefit anyone else. It is a request made purely for Peter's sake, so he can experience a thrill.

Things do not turn out the way Peter imagined they would when he called upon the Lord. It starts out well, but then he gets scared and the whole thing turns into a nightmare. Peter called upon the Lord for his own wants, and instead of getting what he wants, he finds himself sinking, drowning.

There is a strong impulse in us to make the mistake that Peter made in calling upon the Lord. Tony Campolo describes the difference between magic and religion as this: Magic deals with trying to manipulate God, to get God to do what we want God to do. True religion tells us what God has done and is doing and will do for us.

The instant access world is geared for magic. It's geared toward getting what we want, quickly and efficiently. It especially appeals to Christians who are more superstitious than religious. Who view prayer as the magic genie. Who view good works as the way to get in tight with God. Who view worship as the way to manipulate God.

Magic Christians are interested in the transaction, but not in a relationship. They want the goods God has to offer. They want it fast and painlessly. They want God to scan it, bag it, and wish them a nice day, and that's about it. That's not calling on the Lord. Calling on the Lord is not about convenient access for those who think they deserve it. It's about taking time to interact with God. To listen and hear, probe and ponder.

On the other hand, Peter calls upon Jesus a second time in this story. When buffeted by the strong wind, he becomes frightened and begins to sink. Through his own foolishness and recklessness and lack of faith, he is drowning. And so he calls upon the Lord. "Lord, save me!" This time there is no delay. There is no ritual. There's no getting to know each other better. There's no meditation, no reflection. There's action. Instant response. "Jesus immediately reached out his hand and caught him." *Whoever calls upon the Lord will be saved.*

So, isn't this magic religion? Isn't Peter's calling upon the Lord a way for him to get God to do something quick? No, because he did not get Jesus to save him. Jesus was just being Jesus. We don't manipulate God to save us. There are no magic formulas or tricks or persuasive arguments we can use for our benefit. It's a waste of time to barter or bargain with God, to plead or beg. Saving is what God does. That is what God offers, all the time, no matter what you do. When it comes to salvation, to living in relationship with God, call upon the Lord and you will be saved. That's it.

Some of us are suspicious of deathbed conversions. We note sarcastically that there are no atheists in a foxhole on the battlefield. We shake our heads at the common tendency of humans that when all else fails, all we can do now is pray.

But God is all about saving. That's what God does. Salvation is for everyone and far be it from us to deny anyone access to that whether in our theology or our worship. By all means, speed dial

God when you are need of saving. When your life is a wreck, when you are so burdened with pain or anger or fear that you do not know where to turn, dial 911 to God. Because God is all about saving.

What I take from all this is that when we use that saving characteristic of God only as a last resort bailout system, we miss so much of what God has to offer. If we spend more time calling on the Lord in the old-fashioned way, taking some time to meet with God in person, if we would just, in the words of the Psalm, "be still and know that I am God," we wouldn't spend so much time sinking. Just ask Peter.

Chapter 19

I Wonder:
If it's true that we are to "ask and it will be given to you," why don't I get what I pray for?

I once saw an online preview of a basketball game between Oral Roberts University and Memphis State. In analyzing the two teams' relative strengths, the column labeled "intangibles" favored Oral Roberts. The writer's comment was, "Never underestimate the power of prayer." Now I know that was tongue in cheek. But, seriously, in a tense and desperately important game, it is not uncommon to see people turning to prayer. Fans flood the heavens with prayers that the Cowboys miss that field goal, or that their grandson will make that free throw with no time left on the clock.

Have you ever been tempted to pray for divine intervention in a sports game? Apparently some very famous and successful athletes do this all the time. I really wonder about people giving powerful and heartfelt testimonials that God is a corrupt sports bookie who is concerned with fixing the outcome of sporting events. If I did that kind of thing, I would go to jail, but is it okay for God to destroy the spirit of fair play on which athletic competition depends?

When it comes to prayer, a lot of Christians practice and even seem to believe things that are so off the wall it's a wonder that anyone takes Christianity seriously. As much as this grates on me, I have to admit that I have been guilty of this. I don't even want to remember, much less publicly admit, all the goofy things I have prayed for in my life, but I can tell you that a lot of those prayers had to do with locating misplaced items. Where do we get these notions of God as a genie, the granter of wishes? Someone who can influence the future to our benefit if we can just figure out which magic words to say or utter them with the proper urgency and sincerity? When did prayer become the equivalent of wishing upon a star?

It would be silly if it were not so tragic. I once looked out from the pulpit to see two women sitting near each other. Both of those women had had loved ones serving in the armed forces during the war in Iraq, and during the year had repeatedly requested our prayers for the safety of those men. One of the loved ones had returned home safely; the other had been the killed.

Those two were praying for exactly the same thing for their family, with equal passion and devotion, reinforced by the prayers of the congregation. With very different results. I struggled to make sense of this. Did God choose one family over the other one? What are the rules to this prayer game? Is it a popularity contest—whom does God like better? Is prayer an election, and whoever can stuff the ballot box with the most votes, the most prayers wins? Is the God revealed to us in the Bible someone who can say, "Yes, I will grant that request; I will intervene in the world and use my power for this woman to get her parking spot so that she can save 45 seconds and a few steps, but I will ignore that woman's request that she and her brother be spared the agony of his death in combat." Does that describe in any way a divine being of wisdom, justice and mercy?

My wife and I were once invited to participate in a prayer group that kept a running tally of "answered" prayers. Every week, each of the members gave a progress report on the status of their prayers. Yep, they totaled up the hits and misses. To them, God was a very inefficient online shopping network, accessed through prayer, and we keep track of the deliveries and the items that have been back-ordered or sometimes even lost. Where do we get these ideas? You look at a passage from Luke and it seems that Jesus has only himself to blame for the mess we have made of prayer. Doesn't it say right there, "Ask and it shall be given to you?" Didn't Jesus say in Mark, "Whatever you ask for in prayer, believe that you are receiving it and it is yours"? Doesn't that sound like God has an unlimited credit balance for us and prayer is the pin number that gives us access to it?

In studying Luke's passage on prayer more closely, I see God speaking to us in a way that can turn us away from this nonsense and back to what prayer is supposed to be. First, have you ever said to someone who really needs you, "If there's anything I can do for you, anything at all, please don't hesitate to ask?" I'm sure you have; I've said it myself. When someone says that to you, what is your response? "That's great, I would like a new Corvette, a lifetime supply of chocolate, tickets to the Super Bowl, and a secure retirement fund, how about it?"

That kind of response, if it were serious, would damage if not destroy whatever relationship you had with that person. The offer of help was not made lightly. It was a solemn expression of caring. It was meant to let the person know that you will do whatever you can to help them in a time of need. Treating that offer as a blank check is cynically using that person for whatever you can get out of them. Treating Jesus' invitation to prayer in the same way is just as cynical. Jesus' offer is one of caring and relationship; it's not a coupon for a gigantic shopping spree.

Keeping track of "answered" prayer is another way we distort what prayer is all about. Recording answered prayer is basically a public auditing of God's compliance with God's implied contract to give us what we want.

I have a hard time with this concept of "answered" and "unanswered" prayers. During their college years, our children called frequently, and sent us emails. Sometimes they asked for things. Sometimes they did not. Sometimes we could help them out, give them what they asked for; sometimes we couldn't, or chose not to. But we always answered them. I cannot imagine not answering them. It would be very hurtful to imagine them with their little tally sheets, monitoring how well we produced; that their only concern in all that communicating was "did I get what I asked for?"

It is no great leap of faith to say that God answers every prayer. That's a given; that's a promise. What really jumped out at me from this passage in Luke, though, is the conclusion. After saying "Ask and it will be given to you," Jesus concluded this way: "If you, who are far from perfect, know how to give good gifts to your children, how much more will your Father in heaven give the Holy Spirit to those who ask him."

What did Jesus say you would get if you ask? Anything you want? No, it's actually restricted here to one thing: the Holy Spirit. Basically, this says, "Ask in good faith for the Holy Spirit and it will be given to you. Always." Don't ask God to choose sides in a human recreational competition. Don't ask God to choose sides between desperate people. Don't ask God to bankroll your schemes and wishes. Ask for what God promised to give you—a share of God's spirit.

The Lord's Prayer reinforces this truth as plainly as can be. When the disciples asked for an example of how they should pray, Jesus said, When you pray, ask for these things:

Ask for God's kingdom to be with you.

Ask for God's will to be done.

Ask for what you need to get through the day.

Ask for forgiveness.

Ask for strength in times of trial.

Ask that you do not give in to evil.

Those are things that God can give, and God is eager to give. Ask for them and you will receive them. Ask for a vintage Rolls Royce in mint condition and you're going to be disappointed.

So is it wrong to pray for things that we desperately wish for. For ourselves and for others whom we love? No, not if we understand what prayer truly is. Prayer is sharing with God, and sharing means you are free to share your deepest hopes and dreams and wishes and fears. God wants to hear what we think and feel, as individuals and as a group.

Will God make all our dreams and wishes come true? God is

not a genie or a fairy godmother. But God will give us the Spirit, a glimpse into God's kingdom, what we need to get through the day, forgiveness, strength in times of trial, resistance to evil. We will get those things if we ask for them.

It does us good to pray. When we pray the way Jesus taught us to pray, those wonderful things come to us.

It does others good to be prayed for. When we pray the way Jesus taught us to pray, those wonderful things come to others.

It does creation good when we pray. John Polkinghorne speaks of prayer as making sure our will lines up with God's, like the focused light that powers a laser. The more people who pray, the more wills are lined up with God's will, the more God's power can do in the world. The more people who pray a prayer like the Lord's prayer, the more God's will can be done. That's how prayer works.

One of the biggest surprises for me at seminary was that they don't teach you how to pray. As a pastor, I was no "better" at praying than anyone in my congregations. I must honestly admit that the only reason I did so much praying in my church was because it was in my job description. It was expected of me. So I did it, and I found that, surprise, I could.

It is an uncomfortable position for a pastor. It stereotypes us as the designated holy person whom the masses pay to handle the prayers, because the lay people do not think they can do it. I actually had people get upset in one of my congregations if someone other than a pastor uttered a prayer during worship services.

But we don't need intermediaries to talk to God. We really aren't teaching the right thing about prayer if we use them all the time. God doesn't give style points for prayers. Alan Padgett says prayer is really nothing more than a child climbing into God's lap to share some time. If we ask an intermediary to climb into God's lap for us, we are missing the best part about prayer.

Part VI

Questions about Christian Living

Chapter 20

I Wonder:
What is the meaning of life?

When I have asked confirmation students why we are here in this world, two of the three most common responses I got were a bewildered shrug, or some talk about "God's plan." (I'll deal with the third response in the next chapter.)

But even for religious folks, questions about the meaning of existence are not the same as questions about God's plan. Purpose and plan are very different. If I am playing defense against you on a football team, I know what your purpose is: to score a touchdown. But that doesn't mean I have a clue what play you called in the huddle. We cannot play the game of life without knowing what the object of the game is. We have to know, "why am I here?"

One of the most popular spiritual books of recent decades has been Rick Warren's *The Purpose Driven Life*. The reason the book has drawn such a huge audience is because it asks an important question, one on which churches have dropped the ball for so long. We have focused way too much on trying to figure out what plays God is calling, when so many people do not even know what the object of the game is.

Warren stepped up and asked the most basic, most fundamental question of human existence: Why am I here? While I do not agree with all of his answers, I give him credit for asking the question that needs to be asked, and needs to be answered before we can begin to understand what life is about.

The writer of Ecclesiastes certainly wondered about this. What is the point of our existence, asked the preacher. What is the point of life when, in the long run, so much of it does not matter? You can be the best person around, work hard, accomplish goals, win awards, enjoy great relationships, acquire great possessions, and what does it matter in the end? A hundred years from now, who will know? All those things that we thought were so important at the time. Turns out its all vanity; it's all mist. Ecclesiastes then wonders, "Is there any point in life besides grabbing whatever happiness you can, when you can get it? Is that all there is?"

I must have had very weird friends in high school. In most high school yearbooks, friends write encouraging things: thanks for being you, don't ever change, didn't we have great times together? Here's what one of my friends wrote in my senior yearbook, a quote from Shakespeare's Macbeth:

Tomorrow and tomorrow and tomorrow creeps along in its petty pace from day to day until the last syllable of recorded time. Out, out brief candle, life is but a walking shadow, a poor player who struts and frets his time upon the stage and is heard no more. It is a tale told by an idiot, full of sound and fury, signifying nothing.

I don't think he was totally serious, but what is deadly serious is how that little speech sums up so many people's feelings. It is not surprising, because when you take God out of the equation, I don't see where you can come up with any other answer. If God is not part of life then that speech by Macbeth pretty well says it all. There are philosophers who take the evidence of randomness in the evolution of the universe to mean the absence of God. Their answer to "Why am I here?" is that it is just an accident. We are all just victims of fate. There is no meaning. We just are. Grab whatever pleasure you can out of life because nothing ultimately matters anyway. What happens when you believe that? You have no purpose. Life is a tale told by an idiot, full of sound and fury, signifying nothing.

Those agnostic philosophers are right about one thing. Without God, there is no purpose to life. Without God, there is no reason why I am here. It just happened. No wonder so many people in our society today are lost. No wonder so many young people are confused. No wonder there is so much unhappiness. No wonder so many ruin their lives pursuing pleasure whether it be in enormous homes and material wealth, or in endless entertainment, or in alcohol or drugs, or any number of obsessions. If life has no meaning, why not? You may as well do whatever feels good at the time.

There is only one thing to prevent us and the world from going down that gloomy, self-destructive path. We have to believe that there is a purpose to our lives, a reason why we are here. I don't see how that can happen without a connection to a moral force—a connection to God. If God is not an active and present force in the universe, then there is no answer to the question, why am I here?

So, assuming there is an answer, then why are we here?

Psalm 8 takes up the question from Ecclesiastes. When the psalmist looks at all of life, all the beauty and wonder, and all the freedom that humanity has been granted, he is astounded at how much God has given us. God has made us only a little lower than God. Why? Why did God share all that with us? He's stunned by his own answer, which piggybacks onto Ecclesiastes—so that we can enjoy it.

So answer #1, which seems to offend a lot of religious people, is that our purpose is to enjoy the gifts that God has shared. That is what pleases God. That is why Ecclesiastes came to his conclusion that there is nothing better for mortals than to eat and drink, and find enjoyment in their toil. That is the gift that God gave us. Our purpose is to enjoy that gift.

Actually, this is the answer that appeals to almost everyone but religious people. However, it is only a start; there is more to it than that. The core message of the Bible is that the God who makes purpose possible in the world is a giving, sharing being, who has discovered that there is nothing greater in all of existence than the giving of self to another.

Genesis makes a fascinating claim about this. It declares that God decided not only to make beings with whom God could share love, God decided to make those beings in God's own image. That statement about image gives us a strong clue as to what our purpose is. If God's purpose is to share and to love, and we are creatures made in God's image, then our purpose is the same as God's.

Answer #2, then, is that our purpose is to share, to love, to form relationships, to give ourselves in the service of others. As Genesis tells us, when we strive for and accomplish that purpose, it's all good.

There is a third answer that we find in the New Testament. In Matthew 25, Jesus told a parable that spoke directly to the question of "Why am I here?" That is the story of the master who gifts his servants with talents and then looks to see what use they make of them. This parable suggests we are here to use the gifts that God has given us. Our purpose as creatures in God's image, is to create as God creates. Our purpose is to take the gifts and talents that we have been given, and make something out of them.

In summary, my wondering about why we have been given life, has uncovered three reasons:

#1. To enjoy the gifts that God has given us. (Most of us have got this one down pretty well.)

#2. To form relationships in which we can give of ourselves. (Most of us could use some work on this one.)

#3. To use the gifts we have been given for the good of creation.

Those are the objectives of the game of life. I cannot imagine that a loving, giving God is a grasping, control freak who draws up instructions as to how we are to play this game. I think the fun part of sharing life is watching those you love use the gifts they have been given to achieve those worthwhile objectives.

Chapter 21

I Wonder:
Is this life just an audition for the next?

Identifying the meaning of life is not enough for many folks. Both religious and nonreligious folks seem to have this innate competitive desire to win. There should be prizes or awards for those who play the game of life well, and possibly punishment for those who do not. The third common answer I received from confirmation students as to why we are here in this world was that life is a test to see if we deserve eternal life.

I have never been comfortable with the long shadow that Judgment Day casts over the religious. I really have problems with the idea that the purpose of life is to see if you can do it well enough to earn God's approval and the promise of a glorious eternal life. I have even more questions about a loving, giving God who condemns those who are unable to pass the test to a life of eternal torment.

Those questions lead me to examine the last lesson Jesus taught in the Gospel of Matthew. It is one of those Judgment Day scenes; in fact, it's the one referred to in the Apostles' Creed — when it says Jesus shall come again to judge the living and the dead. Since it is the last lesson Jesus taught, it has a sense of urgency about it. What we see here is often described as the ultimate audition. All the nations are gathered here; all those alive, and probably all those who have ever lived, stand there waiting for word on who makes the cut to get into heaven.

My wife and I know all too well from our children's experience in the arts the almost unbearable stress that comes with auditions. It is the same thing that goes on backstage at tryouts for American Idol, The Voice, at NFL football training camps, at auditions for opera or a prestigious orchestra, or even at job interviews.

I don't know how candidates for these positions stand the suspense, the anxiety of hoping against hope to hear their name called. You set your heart on something that could decide your entire future, and you pour yourself into making that dream happen. Now the day of decision has arrived. Here comes the moment of truth that we've all been waiting for: did you make it or not? Take the anxiety of those scenes and multiply it a hundred times. The stakes here are infinitely higher, because we are talking about the ultimate prize: do you make heaven or don't you? Do you get to spend eternity with God, or does the hammer come down and you face the unthinkable alternative? Could we have a drum roll? The envelope please!

This judgment scene does not tell us how the news is broken to the hopeful aspirants. Just that through some lightning round of judgment, the winners and losers are separated. On one side we have the sheep, those who made the cut. On the other we have the goats. They are the ones who get the "we're sorry, you didn't win, but thanks for playing."

Jesus constantly comes up with the unexpected, and do you know what I find absolutely astounding about this scene? It turns out nobody understood the rules. Not the winners, not the losers. In this most crucial of events, on which so much is riding; nobody was clear on what the rules were.

Jesus announces that the division between sheep and goats is based on how you treated Jesus when he was in need. How did you treat Jesus when he was hungry and thirsty? How did you treat him when he was a stranger, when he had no clothing to keep warm, when he was sick, when he was in trouble? In those situations, he says, the sheep treated him well, with mercy; and because of that, they're in. The goats did not, and so they don't make the cut.

The problem is, no one can remember those situations ever happening! Even more perplexing, these are situations that do not make any sense. They are not realistic; they *couldn't* have happened. The risen Lord does not need food or water or clothing. God isn't a stranger; the whole world belongs to God — God is never outside God's own realm. God does not get sick, and almighty God certainly is not going to be incarcerated.

The criteria are so obviously bogus that everyone cries foul. How can you judge us based on something that never happened? What kind of justice is that? It is so unfair that there is something very close to a rebellion going on. Standing before the throne of the Almighty, All-Wise, and Holy Supreme Being, everyone on both sides tosses out the red flag to challenge the decision on the field.

Now we would expect that reaction from the goats. They got the short end of the stick and they have so much to lose. They complain bitterly that they are being condemned for something they did not do. They have lost out on eternal life because of something that never happened. Why weren't they judged on real things, important things, like how much they worshipped God and honored God, and how strongly they believed?

There is a legend about J.C. Penney that when he was hiring someone for a management position, he first took them out to dinner. If the prospective employee salted or peppered any of his food before tasting it, he was eliminated from consideration. The disappointed applicants never saw that coming; they were focused on the important things: poise, competence, experience, résumé. To get the axe because they prematurely salted their potatoes? It seemed so unfair. But Penney's reasoning was that he did not want to hire someone who acted before knowing all the facts.

We seem to have the same situation here. Whatever happened to John 3:16? Whatever happened to baptism and belief in Jesus as the two requirements for eternal life? Isn't that what it's supposed to be all about? Those things *never get brought up here; they are not even mentioned as factors in the decision.* We don't know what the sheep or the goats believed, if anything. There are, no doubt, some very holy people, very religious people among the goats. People with long and impressive résumés in church life. Yet they can't even get a foot in the door because of a hypothetical situation that never happened. So they're not only distraught, they are angry. They feel betrayed. They file a protest. You can't change the rules in the middle of the game, and decide an issue as crucial as eternal life based on some weird criteria that nobody saw coming.

Again, we would certainly expect that kind of reaction from the losers. But isn't it interesting that we get the same baffled reaction from the winners? They do not respond with an outburst of relief and high fives and giddy hilarity at having the ultimate burden lifted from their shoulders. Instead, they stand there opened-mouthed in shock. They don't understand what just happened. You would think they would just shut up and accept their good fortune. *Don't look a gift horse in the mouth. If that's the way Jesus wants to play the game; hey, it worked out well for us so just let it go.*

But they are so bewildered by what's gone on that they just can't keep silent. "What in the world are you talking about?" they ask. "If those are the rules, the requirements, how did we get in? We never saw you in those situations you describe, and we did not do what you said we did." Jesus answers, "When you acted as you did toward the least of those in my family, you did it to me."

What he is saying is, "You've all been around people who have nothing to eat, who are homeless, who are strangers and without friends in the world. You have been around sick people and those in prison. I am in and with every human being on this earth. And I am especially with those for whom life is difficult, with those who are suffering in pain and need. That's where you can best find me. When you show love to those people, you are showing love to me. When you show indifference or disdain for them, you are showing it to me.

This Judgment Day scene is so unsettling because no one saw it coming. Not the sheep, not the goats. Nobody really understood the rules. In other words, no one in this story made it to heaven because they followed the rules so well—because they demonstrated great mastery of the requirements for eternal life. No one in this story was rejected from heaven because of failure to follow the rules. No one lost out on eternal life because they failed to meet the requirements for eternal life.

The sheep got in not because they mastered a set of requirements, but because God changed their lives. They became people who lived in the grace of their Lord. They were living so fully in the goodness of God that it did not occur to them to act any way other than what they did toward their fellow humans.

An old-school pastor told me of the time when he was lectured by a member of the church council that visiting the sick and the troubled was the pastor's job not his. The pastor responded, "I don't visit the sick and the hurting because it's my job. I do it because that's what Christians do." The sheep in this story were not doing what they did in hopes of a reward; in fact they did not even seem to understand that they were going to get a reward for doing it. When they fed the hungry, they were just doing what Christians do.

The goats failed to get in because for one reason or another Jesus was not able to be a part of their lives, and could not change their lives. Many of them were apparently astounded at getting shut out. They may have protested that they worked very hard to please the Lord. While they were not perfect, they certainly were more devout than many of those sheep that got let in.

The issue here is focus and motive. The goats were concerned with trying to impress the Lord. There is a big difference between trying to impress the Lord and living in the Lord. When you try to impress someone, the focus is on the self. The focus is on how high you can raise yourself in the other person's eyes. The focus is on how well you can play the game to get what you want out of the situation. Eternal life is the goal. How well can you impress God so that you can get that benefit?

There was a great scene in the first episode of the television show *The West Wing*, in which Sam Seaborn learns that the daughter of his boss will be visiting the White House along with her school class. Sam is desperate to curry favor with her to earn points with the boss. Although he does not know which one she is, he tries so hard to make a good impression on this school girl while talking to the class that he makes a fool of himself — to the point where the exasperated teacher pulls him out of the room and asks, "Are you a moron?" Sam confesses that he's out to impress his boss's daughter and makes it clear that he is not interested in impressing anyone else, especially not the teacher. Finally, he begs her to tell him which member of the class is his boss's daughter.

The teacher answers, icily: "That would be me." Had he simply acted with concern and compassion for all people, Sam would have impressed the boss's daughter. By having a very narrow and predetermined idea of who she was, he lost sight of her. By focusing so hard on trying to impress her for his own benefit, he lost sight of who he was, and so managed to alienate her.

The goats have been trying very hard to impress God so that they can earn their way to heaven. They have this picture of God as this person who demands sacrifice and rituals and stern and rigid codes of behavior. That is the God they have in mind as they fall all over themselves in their attempts to impress. They think they are impressing God by showing how righteous they are. They think they are impressing God by quoting and teaching pious sentiments. They push aside the hungry and the lost and the weak and the powerless so they can focus on the more important task of impressing God by promoting a "Christian" agenda. They ask with righteous indignation, "Where is God in our society?" And in the fingers of the hungry and the powerless and the hurting—the people they have ignored, God taps them on the shoulder and says, "That would be me."

In this vision of judgment, the people stand there nervously waiting for God to make the call, to divide themselves into sheep and goats. In the end, they find that this eternal life business is not an audition; it is not a prize to be won by impressing God. The Judgment Day in this scene is not what anyone expected. It is not the ultimate turning point. In fact, nothing really changes on Judgment Day. God doesn't make any decisions. It isn't God who creates the division between sheep and goats. The goats have already made that choice. They decided they would rather impress God than live with God.

The message of this story is that there is no audition for eternal life. Eternal life is living with God. The invitation is given to all of us. We either want to be with God or we don't. If we are not interested in living with God on this earth, if we do not like the company God keeps in this world, we show that we are not much interested in living with God. And God accommodates that lack of interest.

The sheep who enter into the joy of the master at Judgment Day discover that they were already living in the joy of their master. The good news for them is in discovering that nothing is going to change on Judgment Day and that, through God's grace, they can continue to live with God forever.

Chapter 22

I Wonder:
Why Do Good People Get Hosed?

My dad used to tell a story about a crowded train traveling in a mountain region. Standing in the middle aisle of the train were a sergeant, a private, and a beautiful young woman. The train went into a tunnel under the mountains and everything was pitched into darkness. Suddenly, there was the sound of a passionate kiss, followed by a resounding slap. Moments later, when the train emerged from the tunnel, the woman looked flustered and angry, and the sergeant had a bright red welt on his cheek.

Everyone left the train that day believing they knew exactly what happened. The passengers all concluded that the sergeant had taken advantage of the darkness to kiss the young woman and had gotten from her what he deserved. The sergeant assumed that the private had kissed the woman who had responded by swinging wildly, and had hit him by mistake. The woman assumed that the sergeant had kissed her and that the private had stepped forward to protect her honor. They were all wrong. Only the private knew what really had happened. He had kissed the woman and then slapped the sergeant.

The truth is not always what we assume. What we know of the facts may be true and yet we find ourselves jumping to conclusions that turn out to be way off the mark. We think we have all the information to reach a correct conclusion, when we don't. This reality lies at the heart of one of the oldest and most wrenching dilemmas in all of Christianity: in a world in which God reigns supreme, why do bad things happen to good people? That question created a best seller and I suspect nearly everyone has wondered about it at some time or other.

One of the standard Christian responses is that God works in mysterious ways and, despite how it may look, everything happens for a reason. In light of the Holocaust and other unspeakable horrors that have taken place in the world, I simply cannot understand how anyone can just shrug off the question of suffering as "it is what it is," something that happens for a divine purpose that we do not fully understand. Because of this, I was fascinated to discover in seminary that the ancient Hebrews wrote a book dealing with this very issue.

The book of Job is a folk tale at its finest. It is a once-upon-a-time story that tells of a man from long ago who was impossibly rich and impossibly good, who suffers impossibly bad luck. At first Job stoically accepts the evil that happens to him as just part of the cost of doing business with God. God is mysterious and unpredictable. You gotta take the good with the bad. But as his misfortunes mount beyond what any human being could possibly endure, he starts to wonder about God. It occurs to him that what is happening to him is a terrible injustice. It is clear to him that he does not deserve this. If God allows such glaring injustice in the world, what does that say about God? There seem to be only two possible options: either God is not loving and just, or God is not all-powerful.

Like so many pious people, Job's friends refuse to go there. They hide behind their religious axioms: God is loving and just and all-powerful. God gives people only what they deserve. Therefore, they conclude from the facts that all the evil that befalls Job must be Job's fault. But the story purposely sets up Job as an impossibly good man just to stop anyone who wants to take that easy way out. Job is so good that he gives offerings to God daily as an apology on the off-chance that his children might have sinned the previous day. There is no way Job deserves what happens to him. Early on, God calls Job "blameless," and in chapter 42, after all the misfortune has occurred, God confirms this. God comes right out and calls Job's friends' liars, and declares that Job was right: the evil that befell Job was not his fault.

Job then comes to what seems to him the logical conclusion to the facts: If the all-powerful Creator of the universe can let such terrible things happen to him, God must not be compassionate or just. Job does not say that in anger. Remember, he is an impossibly good and obedient man. He does not deny that God has the right and the power to do whatever God wants. Job just wishes that God were not so uncaring. But when Job comes to this seemingly logical conclusion, God roars to life. A voice out of a whirlwind slams Job against the wall with a series of pointed questions that say, "Who do you think you are to call me unjust and unloving?"

We discover as we listen to God's speech that God has no quarrel with the facts as Job sees them. Again, God says that Job was right: In no way does Job deserve what has happened to him. Yes, he got hosed, but good. That's right, bad things do happen to good people. What God will not stand for is the conclusion Job draws from this fact. God is not compassionate or just? Do you know nothing about God? Compassionate and just pretty much define exactly what God is. *Job, your conclusion is dead wrong.* Which leaves Job struggling like the rest of us with the question we started with: If God, who is powerful, is also compassionate and just, why does God allow good people to suffer?

God's speech goes on to address that. The answer, Job, is all around you. It is everywhere you look. The answer is tied up in boundaries. *Do you know who made the boundaries of the universe, Job?* God asks.

Uh, you did, squeaks Job.

That's right, says God. *Do you know why I made boundaries? I set boundaries because nothing meaningful comes out of chaos, and I wanted something meaningful to come out of this world that I made. I had to create order, and order means setting boundaries. And so I made the bars and the doors for the sea, and said, "Thus far you shall come and no farther." I set boundaries for the stars and determined their measurements. I set boundaries for the universe.*

Setting boundaries means there are things inside and outside the boundaries. Setting boundaries means there are things you can and cannot do. There are things, for example, that humans cannot do because of the boundary of mortality. Boundaries prevent us from being two places at once. Therein lies the answer to Job's dilemma: because of the boundaries God set to make life meaningful, *there are things God cannot do.*

That conclusion rubs Christians the wrong way. Didn't Jesus say in Matthew 19:26, "With God all things are possible?" Didn't the angel in Luke 1:37 say to Mary, "Nothing is impossible with God?" What do you mean, there are things God can't do?

Let me ask you this: do you truly believe that nothing is impossible for God? Really? Do you believe that it is possible for God to enjoy torturing little children? Do you believe that it is possible for God to lie and deceive? Do you believe it is possible for God to be so shallow that the only thing God really enjoys is a six-pack of beer?

The message of the Bible is that God *cannot* be that way. Those things are impossible for God, not because God could not do them, but because God *will* not do them. God chose to make them impossible, because God chose to establish boundaries of what is possible and what is not. God chose to limit God's self, by making boundaries that even God cannot cross.

Like Job, all of us have a need to figure out who God is, and how God works. We need to understand what the boundaries are. God allows us to do that in two ways: from what God reveals to us in the handiwork of God's creation, and from what God reveals to us in the authority of the Word.

Again, there is too much argument between the religious world and the scientific world about where the boundaries are and what they mean. It does not have to be. Here is what I have found to be a good rule of thumb: if you want to know what the boundaries are that God created for the universe, look to science. God made no secret of what those boundaries are, and gave us the tools to understand them. The fact is we understand those boundaries a great deal better than did the authors of the Bible, because we have better tools than they did.

Again, scientific tools show us that the boundaries that God created are far more wondrous and magnificent than anyone in Old Testament times could have imagined. They did not know that the universe is so huge that as an example of scale, if I place a marble, representing the moon 1 foot away from a softball representing the earth, the nearest of the trillions of stars beyond our solar system would be in Australia.

They did not know there are such things as bacteria, or that there is a kind of bacteria that can live in boiling water. They did not know that God's world includes a single mushroom plant that covers more than 2200 acres. They did not know there is a desert in Chile that hasn't seen a drop of rain in 400 years. They did not know there is really no such thing as a food chain but that all living things form a web of relationship so complex that it is beyond our ability to understand it. They did not know that species are constantly evolving. They did not know that weather systems are so complex that a computer kicking out 2 billion calculations per second cannot make a dent in figuring out all the factors that influence them. Those are the boundaries that God created for the world. Those boundaries are huge and make for a spectacular world, but they are there, and thanks to God's gift of science, we can know many of them.

Knowing the boundaries that God created for God is much more difficult. As God's speech explains to Job, God is larger than the world, and if we think weather systems are difficult to understand, God is infinitely more complex. Yet God is not unknowable. God has made a point of letting us know the important boundaries that God has created for God, at least the boundaries that we need to know about. God reveals those boundaries in the Word.

The Bible tells us that God is bound by promises. God has to keep them, because that is part of God's nature. It tells us that

God is bound by the principles of love and justice and truth. God cannot go against them. That's why God comes down so hard on Job. Job assumed that since God allowed bad things to happen, that God can stray beyond those boundaries of love and justice. He assumed that God is so powerful that God does not have to obey the rules of compassion and justice. That, says God, is simply not true. In the Bible, God tells us, "Whatever else you know about me, never forget this. That you will never find me setting foot outside the boundaries of love and justice. Never."

So, we are still stuck with the paradox. Bad things happen to good people. How can God let these things happen if God is always compassionate and just? Listen to God's answer to Job. Notice again, the answer has to do with boundaries. If God can be bound by love, then God can be bound by other things as well. There are boundaries that have to be created in order for relationship to take place, for life to take place. There can be no life without choice, without change, possibilities, unpredictability, or chance. If God operates and controls everything, existence is meaningless. God's relationship with the world would be like trying to have a relationship with a computer program. God chose to do something more meaningful. God chose true relationship. And, so, God set up boundaries that limited God's power in order to make life and relationship possible. *Because God chose to set boundaries that make life meaningful, there are things God cannot do.*

Job's friends concluded that when tragedy strikes, it's the victim's fault. You are responsible for your pain. For many centuries and even today, Christians have made the same mistake, with devastating results. Job concluded that when tragedy strikes, it's God fault. God is responsible for your pain. Many Christians today make the same mistake, with devastating results.

In the book of Job, God declares that when tragedy strikes, it is because people get caught on the wrong side of boundaries.

If you want to know *why* God set the boundaries exactly where God did, good luck. For nearly three full chapters the voice of God fires a series of questions at Job that all ask the same basic thing: *Do you know why I set the boundaries where I did?* That is not something Job can begin to understand. Nor can we ever know why God set the boundaries where they are.

The message of Job is: don't go jumping to conclusions about what God is or is not doing, about what God should or should not be doing in our lives. There comes a point where you need to trust. We know enough about God from God's created order and from God's revealed Word, to know that God cannot be anything other than good, compassionate, loving, and just. Those are the boundaries we know and understand. We know that God will never cross them.

Whatever other boundaries to God's power exist are there because a good, compassionate, loving, and just God chose to put them there. Knowing that is enough to fill us with joy and thanksgiving in the best of times. And to give us comfort and hope in even the worst of times, knowing that God is working to bring good out of whatever happens to us.

Chapter 23

I Wonder:
If Christianity is the truth, why do Christians fight and disagree with each other?

Luke's story of Lazarus and the rich man is perhaps the most vivid example of God's soft spot for the underdog. It is a disturbing story in many ways. What makes me particularly uncomfortable is that it has seriously caused me to wonder why I wasted my time standing up in the pulpit week after week, or why I bothered to write this book.

Jesus tells a story about a guy right out of *Lifestyles of the Rich and Famous*. He lives in obscene luxury, partying day and night while a man named Lazarus lies at his front gate suffering from a painful disease and hunger. No one helps Lazarus; he dies of starvation. At some point, the rich man also dies; we're not told how.

Now in the afterlife, the wheels of justice have turned. The rich man suffers while the poor man is doing fine. Now it is the affluent one who begs for relief. He is told no relief is possible because there is a huge chasm between where he is and where Lazarus is.

Too late, the rich man finally sees the error of his ways. He pleads for Abraham to send Lazarus to his brothers to warn them so they can avoid his terrible fate. Abraham says, "Been there, done that. They have been warned. They have Scripture and it could not be clearer on this subject."

"I know, I know," confesses the rich man. Remembering how he himself ignored all Scripture, he is pretty sure his brothers are not paying any attention. "But if you try something more dramatic, something that will shock the living daylights out of them, like someone coming back from the dead, they can't ignore that." Abraham says, "If they do not believe Moses and the prophets, neither will they believe even if someone rises from the dead."

Now Charles Dickens would argue with that. The plot of *A Christmas Carol* refutes everything that Abraham just said. Ebenezer Scrooge heard warnings all his life and never paid a bit of attention to them. Just kept on being a miserable jerk. It was only when Marley came back from the dead that he was jolted into changing his obnoxious behavior.

What made me uncomfortable about this Lazarus passage is that I tended to side with Dickens against Jesus on this issue. I was under the impression that the failure of people to listen to Moses and the prophets WAS the reason Jesus came into the world. As Christians we proclaim that someone DID arise from the dead. And there is a lot of evidence that people have listened, that this HAS made a tremendous impact on human kind.

The point of us being in worship, and especially of a pastor standing in a pulpit, is to proclaim that resurrection, the story of a dead person come back to life in the hopes that people will heed that message. And here Jesus says, don't waste your time: if they did not listen to the prophets, they're not going to pay attention to this message from beyond the grave. So if people cannot be persuaded by the Christian message, why do we waste breath delivering it?

As I wondered about this, it occurred to me that the problem is in the word "persuade." Is our purpose to *persuade*, or to *proclaim* and let the Spirit of God work in people? This is a hard thing for a former microbiologist and strong advocate of reason in our spiritual lives to admit: but one message of this story for us today is that if our purpose in being Christian is to persuade others to adopt the Christian faith, or worse yet, our particular version of the Christian faith, we are going to be frustrated more often than not. If the purpose is to proclaim the coming of the reign of God in the world, well, that's something else altogether.

Persuasion is highly overrated. For a long time, I have been bewildered by the huge disconnect between facts and opinions in our world, which seems to grow every day. When you spend 20 years of your life researching facts, and then hear how haphazardly people use those facts or reject them or purposely skew them, it makes you want to weep.

I occasionally receive emails that are intended to be a battle cry to Christians everywhere. I remember one article that told how the Obama administration and the ACLU had teamed up to ban the use of crosses on the graves of U.S. veterans at national cemeteries. Not only are they no longer allowing crosses on new gravestones, but they are removing crosses from current gravestones as a means of enforcing separation of church and state. Enough to make your blood boil, isn't it?

Well, it might be except that I knew from personal experience this claim is a bald-faced lie. I had recently buried both parents at Fort Snelling national cemetery. One of the first questions the administration asked was what you would like on the stone, and they offered dozens of versions of the cross to choose from. It has been well documented that every claim in the article is false. Yet email campaigns like this will not die. This one has been circulating for well over a decade and is still going strong. In our internet age, facts mean shamefully little. False information gets spread wider and wider, believed and taken to heart by thousands if not millions of good, honest people, and there is no way to stop it.

I have often wondered why good, intelligent people can come to such opposite conclusions on so many issues. Why are we so polarized in our society? Why is it that every time one group sees red, the other party sees blue? Facts are facts, so how can it be that no matter what anyone proposes in our government, the other side *always* sees it as wrong?

A book called *Mistakes Were Made (But Not By Me)* by Carol Tavris and Elliot Aronson, provides a fascinating clue. Because of something called cognitive dissonance, facts really are not all that important to us. Cognitive dissonance is the painful difference between what we are and how we act. We each have a concept of ourselves that assures us we are basically a good, competent person. Yet each of us does and says things that a good, competent person would not do or say or believe. The logical conclusion is that we are not always good, competent people. But believing ourselves to be bad or incompetent is destructive. It's difficult to live a happy, contented life under that belief. So how do we square this image of ourselves as good and competent with evidence that does not support that? The most common solution is to protect our self-image at all costs. Our minds create elaborate defenses to convince us that we are good and competent, and that evidence to the contrary is wrong. So when we form an opinion, those defenses begin to build a protective wall. The longer we hold an opinion, the stronger that wall becomes.

New information that challenges our words or actions and threatens to show we are wrong is a threat to our self-image. Our cognitive dissonance defense mechanisms protect us by filtering out evidence that we are wrong and by determining that any evidence that does not coincide with our beliefs is fake news. Not being aware this is happening, we do this while believing ourselves to be rational and objective.

Two people can begin with almost identical ideas about, say, immigration. If one begins to lean slightly one way and the other leans just slightly the other way, cognitive dissonance will carry them in different directions. Their defenses will begin to filter out evidence contrary to their initial opinion. This will cause each of them to become more and more strongly entrenched in their opinions. As this happens, more and more facts are filtered out until eventually no preponderance of fact in the world can possibly get through to change their minds.

Christianity offers a life-giving solution to the problem of cognitive dissonance, but it is not a popular one: we confess that we are not perfect, that despite our best intentions, we screw up. This is not self-flagellation or debasing ourselves as unworthy worms. It is a confession of reality, after which we ask God to forgive us, accept God's forgiveness, and try to do better.

Jesus' story of Lazarus and the rich man is a beautiful illustration of cognitive dissonance. The rich man views himself as a good and upright person. Evidence emerges that he is not all that good. His actions toward his neighbor are nothing short of shameful. The law of Moses and the words of the prophets, which he purports to believe, condemn his inactivity. *Do unto others as you would like them to do to you. You will reap what you sow. Love your neighbor as yourself. The moral arc of the universe is long but it bends toward justice. Blessed are the downtrodden of the world.*

Yet he is unmoved by all that. He does not hear any of it. It never registers with him because his defenses have filtered it out. The facts that get through to him are that he is good to his friends and family. He is compassionate; after all he does not call the police on this vagrant. He has earned his position in life, his wealth and luxury, through hard work and ability. God means for us to enjoy the blessings of life and that is what he's doing. As for Lazarus, well, God helps those who help themselves. At this point, what could possibly change his mind? A reminder of God's love? The story of Jesus dying for us and rising from the dead? Testimony means nothing at this point. Facts mean nothing. They all get filtered out.

In the end, the rich man learned the painful reality of those facts that his defenses blocked. Too late, he wants to send some persuasion to his loved ones back on earth so they can avoid his fate. Jesus says, that will not work. Once you are set in your ways, facts don't make a lot of difference. How about a miracle? says the rich man. They will believe a miracle. No, says Jesus, if cognitive defenses can filter out facts, they can easily explain away a miracle. You cannot persuade people of the truth of love that God intends for the world.

So why do I bother to get into a pulpit or to write this book? I have found that I can do it only because I have learned that my primary job is not to persuade but to proclaim. I suspect many of us have frustrating conversations with people, even loved ones, who we feel just do not get it regarding what we understand as the Christian message. Facts and testimony will not work; their minds are made up. I hear Jesus saying in this passage, if you encounter people, whether friends or strangers, who tell you how dumb your beliefs are, you can argue if you want, but it won't do any good. So I do use facts and persuasion, but recognize that they are useful only to people who are open to them. I use them with people of faith to strengthen their faith, to inspire, and comfort.

For people who do not seem to get it, all I do is proclaim. Because what is it that brings unbelievers into true harmony with God? What brings people to the new life that Christ proclaimed? One thing: a change of heart.

The rich man never experienced that. He wants to send a warning back home, but he still does not have a clue what God's kingdom is all about. Even when he experiences the painful consequences of ignoring God, he still doesn't get it because his heart never changes. Listen to what he says. *Send Lazarus to carry some water over here. Send Lazarus back to my brothers.* His attitude never changed. He still has no respect for Lazarus. Even when he is standing in hell and Lazarus ends up in heaven, he thinks he is superior to Lazarus. To him, Lazarus is still a nobody whom he can order around at will. Even to the end he is concerned only for his own welfare and for his family's. He's trying to manipulate others to get a better deal for himself.

So what good will it do to send anyone back to the family? The rich man has experienced the message as close up and as firsthand as you can get, and he still does not get it. And he will not until he has a change of heart. Neither will anyone unless they have a change of heart. Remember that the rich man is told that no relief is possible for him because there is a huge chasm between Lazarus and him. Who created that chasm? Not God; it's there because the rich man created it. He is the one who put distance between himself and Lazarus in his life. Even in his torment, he continues to put distance between himself and that miserable lucky stiff, and because of that, there is no bridging it.

The rich man is not condemned beyond redemption in this story. There is a way out if only he would take it. What is the alternative to the life-destroying, truth-destroying cycle of cognitive dissonance? All he has to do at any point in the story is confess that, despite his best intentions, he screwed up, ask God to forgive him, accept that forgiveness, and live a new life in the light of what he has learned from God.

That requires a change of heart. Something has to break through the delusion created by that wall of self-deception. Something has to change to bridge the gap between ourselves and what God intends. The best chance of that happening has to do with making a connection with God.

Facts cannot change a heart.

Logical argument won't change a heart.

Eloquence won't change a heart.

Sincerity won't change a heart.

Miracles won't change a heart.

I can't change a heart.

It was not Marley coming back from the dead that turned Scrooge around. Nothing would have changed in his life if his heart had not been touched with compassion for Tiny Tim.

God can change hearts. So we proclaim the love of God. We lay it out there in word and deed what God has done for us, and we pray for hearts to change. We pray that the spirit of God can work through our proclamation to pierce the shield of self-deception, change lives, and dissolve the chasm that divides us from God's intended creation. We proclaim the love of God and we pray *your will be done on earth as in heaven*. We proclaim and pray in confidence that will happen.

Chapter 24

I Wonder:
Whose idea was the hard sell in evangelism?

When I was in seventh grade, my school introduced me to the wonderful world of the magazine fund-raiser. They made it sound so good and so easy. All I had to do was go around and show people the tremendous deals they could be getting on these magazines that everybody wants—deals that only I was authorized to give—that would save them a ton of money. Use the ready-made, paint-by-the-numbers sales pitch that they gave me, and the magazines would sell themselves. They baited the hook with these incentives that sounded too good to be true. All I had to do was sell a piddling number of magazines and I would win these incredible prizes. Even though it is not at all my personality, I was eager to get started, so I could sell as many magazines as possible and collect these great prizes.

I started off at the next door neighbor's house. They were not close friends but it was a family we knew well and they had always been nice to me. This sale would be a slam dunk. Still, this whole sales concept was so far outside my comfort zone that my knees were shaking as I started in on the sales pitch. I wasn't halfway through when I was interrupted and told, with a smile, "I'm sorry, we really aren't interested."

That was the end of my sales career. I did not handle rejection well. I felt like an idiot. I went home devastated, my innocence destroyed. I tossed the materials away and never approached another person with my tremendous magazine offers.

If you can relate to that story at all, you probably have some misgivings about the whole notion of evangelism. You may have even more misgivings if you have ever been on the receiving end of a visit from someone who wanted to convert you. Admit it, you squirm when you see them coming in pairs down the block, making their way toward your house, and you quickly make it look like you are not home. Or worse, the doorbell rings and you make the mistake of answering it before you see, oh great, it's them! Maybe you feel just a little guilty because they are such fine, courageous, God-loving people and they are out there doing what we ought to be doing if we were not so timid about our faith.

I read the Gospel story about Jesus sending out a 70-man-strong mission force and it makes me feel uncomfortable, because doesn't it seem that those door-to-door folks we consider so annoying are doing exactly what Jesus expects? Not only do we fail to do what Jesus asks, we cannot stand it when other people do. What does that say about us?

I can't help it; this kind of stuff rubs me the wrong way. Since the passage from Luke 10 is probably the basis for door-to-door Jesus-selling campaigns, it's a good idea to ask some questions about it.

People often assume Jesus had only 12 disciples, but this passage and others show us that his following was much greater. There was a small group of 12 that had some special jobs to do, some special responsibilities. But there were many other followers, many of whom are not known to us, who also followed Jesus, and they did their share to chip in where they were called. This episode is a case where they are called into action.

After explaining to his followers how urgent the mission is, Jesus appoints a large number of his followers to undertake a task. "The harvest is plentiful and the laborers are few," he says, as he sends them out. The key to this story is, what is the task that Jesus asks them to undertake? What exactly is the harvest they are supposed to achieve?

The first answer that jumps to mind, given our experience with this sort of thing, is that the harvest is souls. The disciples' mission is to win converts to the cause; to convince people of the error of their ways and make them see the light.

Here is where the guilt comes in because if this is the point of the story, then it follows that this is what *we're* supposed to be doing. Beating the pavement, knocking on doors, passing out tracts of religious doctrine, ringing up sales for Christ. Winning trophies for the heavenly mission case.

But it may be a relief to your blood pressure to learn that this is not what the passage says. Look again at what Jesus says these disciples are supposed to be doing when they enter a town on this harvest mission:

Verse 5: Share the peace.

Verse 7: Live among strangers.

Verse 9: Heal the sick.

Verse 9: Proclaim the coming of God's kingdom.

That's all. It says nothing about harvesting souls. It says nothing about winning converts. It says nothing about trying to make sales for Jesus. It does not say those things because that is not what the life of Jesus Christ was about. He did not see people as objects of conquest, but as people made in God's image, people in need of love and new life.

Paul sums up what the harvest is all about on this mission trip in Galatians. "Let us not become weary in doing good," he writes, "for at the proper time we will reap a harvest if we do not give up."

Paul says we will reap a harvest if we do not become weary of what? Of proselytizing? Weary of selling Jesus? Weary of winning souls for Christ? No, Paul says if we do not become weary in doing good, we will reap the harvest. Doing good is what reaps the harvest.

So what *is* the harvest? The harvest seems to be all the potential for good that God has provided in the world. Potential for living and sharing in the glory of God. Potential for peace and prosperity and love and new life. That is what Jesus came to bring into the world.

Jesus said the laborers are few. Does that mean too few laborers out there hitting the pavement to win converts? Or too few laborers out there doing good?

If I am reading this correctly, Jesus says there are too few people sharing the peace, too few living among those who are not like them, too few healing the hurts of the world, and too few who are out there giving people hope by sharing the Gospel story. The harvest of creation is great, the potential is there, if we can just get enough of us out there doing these things.

What about that labor shortage that Jesus mentioned? If the laborers are few, isn't one of our tasks to remedy that by recruiting more laborers?

All I can do is go by what Scripture tells me. And in this passage what does Jesus say he wants the disciples to do about the labor shortage? Listen again to Jesus' words: *The harvest is plentiful, but the laborers are few. THEREFORE ask the Lord of the harvest to send out laborers into the harvest.* Jesus leaves the recruiting of laborers to God.

When we do what Jesus asks us to do on our mission in life—when we share the peace, when we get to know others who are not like us, when we care for those in need, and when we tell the gospel news of Jesus Christ—then God will have no problem getting laborers.

I will never forget the words of a member of my former congregation, a person who had been badly burned by churches who had promised more than they could deliver. She had just about decided to ditch the whole religious scene before she wandered into our church. During one discussion, I started getting a little assertive about a particular doctrine. She pulled me up short, and reminded me:

"I walked into, stayed, and joined this church because there was a person in there who was just being a person and not selling me Jesus flowers."

Too often, we think of evangelism as selling Jesus. As I

read the Gospels, Jesus never sold anything. He never set out to win souls or to see how many people he could convert. He set out to love people and to heal them, and to give them new life. Whatever he had that was of value—and he had plenty—he simply gave away. That is exactly what he asked the disciples to do on this mission: just be a person and not a sales rep:

Share the peace.

Live among strangers.

Heal the sick.

Proclaim the coming of God's kingdom.

He did not ask these disciples to sell anything; he told them to give those things away.

How are we to give those things away today? Here are a few examples I have come up with:

Share the peace. Do not just co-exist with others. Actively pursue peace by whatever means you can. Be the ones to initiate. No, not everyone is going to respond or reciprocate. But many will who otherwise would not have done so if someone did not take the first step.

Live among the stranger. Do not impose your culture or way of life on others. Don't lecture people from afar on what they ought to be doing, or talk about their faults. Spend some time in their houses, walk in their shoes. Accept their hospitality. Eat with them. Look at life from their point of view. Find out what are their needs and fears and hopes.

Heal the sick. Once you have found out what their needs and fears and hopes are, do something about it. Do things for others. See what you can do to bless people, to make their lives better, to make them full participants in the glory of God's creation.

Proclaim the coming of God's kingdom. In word and deed, bring to people the good news that there is a God who is powerful beyond imagination, and that this God loves what God has created, including you.

Jesus said, "Go and make disciples of all nations." But we

don't make disciples by selling anything. We don't make them by targeting converts or winning souls. We don't make them by recruiting workers. Evangelism—proclaiming the gospel—does not require door-to-door cold-calling sales. When a faith community is alive and active and energized and focused on discipleship, then evangelism, part four of Jesus' training manual for mission, is the easiest thing in the world. All it consists of is saying to those around you, "You should see what God is doing in our church!" That is how you proclaim the coming of God's kingdom.

I cannot think of a better way of fulfilling the demands of discipleship outlined in this passage than in the mission trip. Mission trips change people. They change lives. They make disciples. Virtually everyone I talk to who has been on a mission trip comes away saying that was a highlight of their spiritual life; that was where they experienced what Christianity is all about. Why do mission trips like this work? Because they focus on what Jesus told us to focus on in a mission trip.

On a mission trip, we share the peace. We come with no motive other than love and friendship; most of the time, that peace is not only returned, it is returned tenfold.

We live among the strangers. Those on mission trips do not impose their culture or standards on others. They live as their hosts live; eat as their hosts eat; experience life as they live. For our congregation traveling to Tanzania, that meant learning to regard water as a precious resource, to be used sparingly. We gain wisdom and compassion by seeing how others live.

We heal those in need. All good mission trips have a huge service component. While there may be fun and adventure built in, we don't go on them to be entertained; the purpose is to do our part to help those in need.

We proclaim the coming of the reign of God. We go not as a club or social group with a philanthropic bent; we go as disciples of Christ. We go as people whose lives have been changed by the good news of the Gospel.

There's a difference here between selling Jesus and proclaiming good news. Yes, we believe we have a great product. Yes, we are passionate about it. And yes, there's a sucker born every minute, so we probably could make some sales. But it is not the calling of a Christian to sell anything. Our call is to give away the love of God that has been given to us free of charge.

I don't know, maybe a sales job can change a life. But I know for certain that a person just being a person and giving away the gospel and its message of love and new life, free of charge, no strings attached, has a better chance of changing lives.

Christ's church will flourish when we realize that we are all on a mission trip in which we:

Share the peace.

Live among strangers.

Heal the sick.

Proclaim the coming of God's kingdom.

That's what Jesus asks his disciples to do. "Let us not become weary in doing good, for at the proper time we will reap a harvest if we do not give up."

Chapter 25

I Wonder:
Wouldn't humanity be better off without religion?

In an earlier chapter, I tried to imagine a universe without God and found I could not do it. The universe simply could not exist without God, and in fact it makes no sense without the very God we encounter in the Bible. God has come to us in power and love and wisdom and faithfulness in the workings of the universe God created.

That leads to a more painful task, trying to imagine a *society* without God. Actually, imagining a society without the God of the Bible is not hard to do. We are quite familiar with such societies; they have existed since the dawn of time. Some of the most powerful empires of early history, including the mighty Roman Empire, seemed to get along, at least for a while, without God, although they did worship deities after a fashion.

Such societies exist today. The most populous nation in the world, China, remains largely a biblical God-free society. In countries all over the globe, indeed in many areas of the United States, you can interact with a huge segment of the population without ever encountering God. You can live virtually your whole life as if God did not exist. Even those who believe in God often banish God to solitary confinement in a gothic prison, with visiting hours restricted to Sunday morning. A *universe* without God would be a chaotic nightmare. But for many people, a *society* without God is not a nightmare but a dream.

That's what the song "Imagine" is all about. Those of my generation surely remember that hauntingly beautiful composition by John Lennon. It asks us to imagine the absence of religion, among other things, and suggests that without it, we would all be living life in peace. In the song, Lennon expressed a hope that we would all join in this religion-free dream of his.

Lennon is not alone in this dream. For many people, eliminating religion and even God from society is the goal. One of the most popular and articulate of these people today is a writer named Sam Harris. Listen to what he has to say, as he dreams of a society without God:

Atheism is nothing more than a commitment to the most basic standard of intellectual honesty: Pretending to be certain when one isn't—indeed, pretending to be certain about propositions for which no evidence is even conceivable—is both an intellectual and a moral failing. Only the atheist has realized this. The atheist is simply a person who has perceived the lies of religion and refused to make them his own.

Once we get past the shock of such statements, we find that there is nothing wrong with most of the goals of Lennon and Harris. Like all of us in our best moments, they are searching for a peaceful and just world. They see religion as one of the greatest barriers to peace and justice in the world. If you look at the evidence of history, you can see where they are coming from.

During the Crusades of the past millennium, huge armies marched thousands of miles to fight endless wars with an enemy who threatened them in no way, because of their religious beliefs. In the seventeenth century, millions of Germans, perhaps as many as a third of the entire population, were killed for no other reason than that their Christian beliefs were slightly different than those of their neighbors. In our country, the Bible was used as the prime justification for a cruel and inhuman system of slavery.

So much of the unrest and violence in the world today, from the Catholics and Protestants of Northern Ireland, to the Sunnis and Shiites and Jews and Christians of the Middle East has its roots in religion. Thinking in terms of human survival, can you think of any motive other than religion that would induce intelligent, educated humans to commit such an insane, murderous act as to slam a jet liner into a high-rise building, killing 3000 people?

Imagine that this motivation did not exist. Imagine a world with no religion, no irrational, fanatical beliefs, no hypocrisy, no one acting as God's privileged favorites, as instruments of God's wrath. Wouldn't a world without God be a more peaceful world?

After seriously and honestly pondering this question, I have come to conclude it would not. Eliminating God from our society would not eliminate the stupidity and short-sightedness that mire society in hopeless futility. Ironically, the campaign to exorcise faith from our world is a prime example of that very short-sightedness. Using the logic and reason so prized by such anti-religion advocates, the argument for banishing God from our society is silly. The overwhelming testimony of the universe is that our world was created by a God who is powerful, loving, faithful, and wise beyond our comprehension. How can that God suddenly become such a hapless bumbler when it comes to human societies that the only solution is for humans to engineer a hostile takeover of God's creation before God wrecks everything? Maybe a little human arrogance going on there!

Does the desire to follow God often cause violence, intolerance, hatred, sorrow, and injustice? Obviously. Does that mean we would be better off if God were eliminated from our world? Not by any logic I know.

Water causes flooding, tsunamis, and tidal waves that kill hundreds, even thousands of people every year. Water causes accidental drownings. It floods basements, leaks through roofs, destroys property. It turns to ice and snow on the highways, creating a dangerous hazard that causes many fatalities. It erodes good farmland. Thousands of people get sick and many die from drinking contaminated water. Water creates boundary disputes between those who want to control it. As clean water becomes scarcer in the future, wars will be fought over water.

Would it be a greater, more peaceful world if there were no water? No, without water, there would be no life. Wouldn't this be a greater, more peaceful world without God? No, without God, there would be no life.

True, if you take God out of the mix on the world stage, you eliminate some destructive behavior on the part of humans who misuse religion. But let's see what else you eliminate. What would this dream society without God really look like? As noted, there would be no meaning to life. Without God, we are an accident. We have no purpose. We have no reason to do anything at any given moment except what makes us happy. The only point to living is to stimulate pleasure neurosensors in the brain as often as possible. If the whole world lived that way, would the world be a better place?

There would be no right and wrong. Without some conception of God, there are no moral absolutes. Torture of small children is as acceptable an activity as showing compassion to the poor, even more so if it gives you pleasure. Enslaving a nation is as fine a goal as providing humanitarian aid. Using weapons of mass destruction is as noble a venture as finding a cure for cancer.

Without God, there would be no stewardship, no reason to care for the earth. Use it, exploit it, and throw it away. There is no reason to preserve anything for anyone else, because no one else matters but me, and I'm not going to be around that long.

There would be no love. Without God, there is no reason to do anything for anyone else. Secular humanists will argue with this and say that there is such thing as the common good. It is to our benefit to cooperate. Individuals benefit when all benefit, and that's why we do things for other people. But that is not love, that is merely bartering. Swapping something to get something.

Love is something different. Lennon tried to separate God from love, but you cannot do it. God is where love comes from; there is no rational explanation for its independent development among humans. Eliminate God and you lose the connection with love, and when that happens, eventually you will lose any understanding of what love is.

When we lose the understanding of what love is, anything can happen. A society without God easily evolves into cruel regimes like Nazi Germany, Cambodia's ruthless Pol Pot, and the colorless, oppressive governments of Communist Europe during the Cold War. Imagine a world without meaning, a world without any sense of right or wrong, a world without stewardship, a world without love. That is what a society without God looks like. I wish it weren't so easy to imagine.

Christians argue that God came to us in the human form of Jesus because, despite the clear evidence overflowing in creation, people lose sight of God. Some think they can build a pure society by killing and oppressing and hating and punishing in God's name. It doesn't happen, because you can do that only by losing sight of God. Some think they can build a wonderful, harmonious society without God. It doesn't happen. A society that loses sight of God is always a bleak place.

The Christmas story shows us exactly what purpose looks like. It shows us what morality looks like, what stewardship looks like, what love looks like. It tells of God coming in such a way that the world would never forget. God came so that even when we lapse into stupidity, shortsightedness, and selfishness, we would have the light shining from a little manger in a stable to pull us back from the darkness of a world we created for ourselves, a world without God.

Chapter 26

I Wonder:
What would my life look like without God?

I am going to ask you to join me in undertaking a very daunting task. We are not going to do it as an intellectual exercise. We are no longer asking the theological questions about where was God in the creation of the universe, or where is God in the mystery and order of the cosmos, and could it exist without God? We are no longer asking where God is in society and whether our culture or nation can survive without an understanding of, and relationship with, God. The question to ask now is up close and personal: What would *my* world be like in the absence of God?

I wish this question were as theoretical as those other questions about God and creation, or God and society. I wish this subject were way beyond my ability to comprehend. That it was so foreign a concept that I could not even speak about it with any degree of authority. But, sadly, it turns out this subject calls for even less imagination than the previous chapter.

Based on the number of encounters I have had with despairing people I suspect many of you have peered over the edge into the dark void that surrounds that question. You may be living in its shadow right now. Because there are times in life when it is difficult to find God. There are times when sorrow and pain make it difficult to see any light. The shadow that hides God from view may be especially long and deep during the holidays, when everyone else is celebrating and partying and rejoicing, filled with a light-hearted warmth that we don't feel. In the midst of that, some of us feel all the more trapped in despair and estranged from God's blessing.

There were Psalmists who peered into the darkness and considered the possibility of living a life in which God was totally absent. Psalm 88 is not a psalm you ever hear on Sunday morning. It's a little too edgy for most Christians. It was written by someone so overwhelmed by pain or fear or sorrow or loss that he was really having trouble seeing the presence of this loving God in his life.

For my soul is full of troubles.

I am like those who have no help, like those forsaken among the dead, like those whom you remember no more.

I am shut in so that I cannot escape, my eye grows dim through sorrow.

Wretched and close to death from my youth, I suffer your terrors. I am desperate.

Your wrath has swept over me; your dread assaults destroy me. They surround me all day long.

The Psalmist is staring at the very real possibility that a loving and compassionate God does not exist, and that therefore he is stuck in this world without the comfort of a God who cares.

Even Jesus reached a place where it took very little imagination to consider a world without a caring God. The words he spoke when hanging on the cross on that Good Friday, probe that very ground: "My God, my God, why have you forsaken me?"

I do not pretend to know what it feels like to peer over the edge into the darkness of a world without God. Thus far I have been spared that. But I can draw a very detailed picture of that darkness, because I have seen it, up close and personal.

In my second year of ministry, I received a phone call from a doctor who told me about a patient with a story to break your heart. He had just met with this woman who I am guessing was in her fifties, a woman dying of cancer. To make matters worse, Alberta had also suffered a stroke that greatly limited her abilities. That is a sober enough beginning to her story, but it gets far worse. This woman had no family other than a sister who lived far away, whom she had not seen in many years. She had no church home; she was not raised in any faith. This doctor asked her if she would like to see a pastor or a priest, and she indicated that she would. For some reason that he was at a loss to explain, she requested an ELCA Lutheran pastor, and so the call came to me.

When I went to visit her, I saw all too clearly what my life would be like without God. I found her alone in her room, lying in a fetal position on her bed in the nursing home. As I sat beside her, she looked at me with an expression that haunts me to this day, an expression of pain, bewilderment, and utter hopelessness. I saw in that expression someone who had given up trying to hold on to her last shred of dignity. Her shirt was soiled with splotches of vomit, which I discovered was not uncommon because her illness had left her largely unable to move. Swallowing was so difficult and painful that it was hardly worth the effort to her; and when she did, the result was often what I saw.

I tried to speak with her, to find out some things about her, only to discover that the stroke had robbed her of that function. She could only, with great difficulty, nod or shake her head. And so the many questions I wanted to put to her went unasked. Because she could answer only yes or no questions, I will never know why she wanted a Lutheran pastor to visit her, or how her life came to be the way it was. She confirmed what the doctor had told me. She had no family. No church. She shook her head when I asked if she had any friends. Through nods and shakes she told me that she had lived in this town for virtually her entire life, and had no important connection to anyone. Perhaps it was the pain and depression talking; but based on the handful of people that came to her funeral, almost exclusively health care-givers, I suspect it was true. She told me she knew nothing about God, or Jesus, or the Christian faith. She told me that she was terrified of the death that was fast closing in on her.

This picture I have just presented to you is very close to a picture of what you or I would look like without God. There is only one act of imagination needed to complete the picture.

Take her out of the nursing home, where the staff, reflecting the love of God, tried to make her as comfortable as they could. Put her alone in a dark, cold apartment, or in a makeshift cardboard shelter in an alley. That is what you or I would look like in a world without God.

It was not in the unfortunate string of illnesses that she found herself separated from God. I have seen how God is able to be present with people in the most difficult of health circumstances. It was in the utter aloneness, the fear, the bewilderment, and most of all, the hopelessness that she lived apart from God. When things are terrible, and getting worse, and you cannot visualize any possible circumstance or event that could ever make that better, that is a portrait of living without God.

When you have no one in your life, neither family nor friends, who care whether you live or die, when your existence seems to have gone unnoticed and you think that your passing away will not make a speck of difference to anyone in the world, that is a portrait of living without God. When you are convinced that life is nothing but an accident, and when that open grave staring you in the face calls you into the icy grip of the grim reaper and not God, that is a portrait of living without God. That is the picture that Jesus came to obliterate from the face of the earth.

Listen to the words of the prophet Isaiah:

The people who walked in darkness have seen a great light.

For a child has been born for us and he is named Wonderful Counselor, Mighty God, Everlasting Father, Prince of Peace.

His authority shall grow continually and there shall be endless peace for the throne of David and his kingdom.

He will establish and uphold it with justice and with righteousness from this time onward and forevermore.

The passage is telling us that God came to us in the person of Jesus to get close to creation. To seek and to save the lost. It tells us that the events of Christmas and Easter occurred to make certain that in the worst of times as well as in the best, each one of us has someone who can touch us with the hand of love and compassion, someone with whom we can share the life-giving gifts that God showered upon us.

God broke into our world to destroy the bleak portraits of emptiness. Jesus appeared in a stable, as a little baby, so that everyone on earth would have the one ingredient necessary for life: hope. Imagine your life without hope, and you will see what your life looks like without God. Hope is the one thing we cannot live without, whether we live in the empty shell of luxury, suffer through the horror of a country torn by violence, fight a losing battle against disease, or find ourselves crushed by grief.

In those moments when we lose hope, and we slide toward the emptiness of a lonely, dark corner, the love of God can bring it back, often through family and friends, sometimes acquaintances and even strangers. That is the way it's supposed to work.

The events of Christmas occurred to make certain that in the worst of times as well as in the best, each one of us is surrounded by hearts and hands of love and compassion. Jesus came to us to show us what love is all about, so that no one would have to end their life alone, in a dark corner. So that no one would be without hope. So that no one would be without God. God's work is not finished until that happens. And so it seems to me the job as people of faith is not finished until that happens. We tell the story, and we carry the message of hope into all the dark places of the world.

Because of that first Christmas in Bethlehem, I was able to visit this woman on Christmas Day, and on behalf of our congregation bring a ray of hope to a person living a razor's width away from a world without God. To let her know how it feels to be special in God's eyes, to have a song dedicated to her in a house of worship. She was not able to see what happened in our congregation, or hear it, but she was able to imagine it. And that is what Christmas does to us.

If you have ever stared over the edge into the abyss of life without God, or if you are living in the shadow of that darkness right now, please accept this gift. May the hope that we share be the lifeline that sustains each of you in your walk through life.

This is the poem that I dedicated to Alberta and read to my congregation with my daughter playing, ironically, "Imagine" in the background. This is what Alberta grabbed hold of at the end instead of the empty outstretched hand of the grim reaper.

Imagine there was no Christmas,
My life without a ray of hope.
Lying in pain in a deep, dark pit.
No one there to throw me a rope.
Imagine all the broken people,
Living without God.

Imagine a drafty stable,
A baby crying on the hay.
God has come into our world,
 With the promise that God will stay.
Imagine all the people
Singing, "Peace on earth."

You may think that I'm a dreamer.
Well, dreams are seeds of what could be.
I hope some day you can join us,
To watch the seed grow to a tree.

Imagine the lame leaping for joy.
A feast grows from every crumb.
Imagine every sunset
Brings a promise of life to come.
Imagine all the people,
Singing, "Joy to the world!"

You may think that I'm a dreamer,
But those dreams are God's seeds of what will be.
I hope some day you'll join us,
And the world will be set free.

Chapter 27

I Wonder:
What if I lose my faith?

I have often heard the expression "clinging to faith." I suspect the fear of losing one's faith is a main reason why so many people are afraid to wonder about faith and to ask questions. Far safer simply to accept whatever faith you have been granted and don't mess with it.

I have already written about what I think of this timid and lifeless view of faith. Nonetheless, I know from where the anxiety comes. There have been times in my life when I have seriously wondered if any of my Christian beliefs make any sense. That is an extremely uncomfortable feeling for one who has been brought up in the faith and, I am certain, for those who have come to faith more recently. It seems like we are flirting with utter annihilation and why would any sane person do that?

It's not because we want to question our faith—in fact we may be terrified of doing so. But in our most honest moments, we confront the possibility that what we so fervently believe may prove to be an illusion. How do we deal with this? What if we find ourselves losing our grip on faith? What if it gets even worse? What if I lose my faith?

When these questions have gnawed at me, I have found that the best response has come out of my experience in the previous chapter with that essential ingredient of life known as hope. In 1 Corinthians, Paul states that Christianity rests on three pillars: faith, hope, and love. Christians have no argument with two of the items on that list. Love is the basis of who God is. Faith is something that churches talk about all the time.

I have heard many sermons and testimonials on the importance of faith and love. Outside of funerals, I cannot remember hearing as much about the importance of hope. It makes me wonder what hope is doing on God's A-list of necessities—until I read passages like this from Revelation 21:

God will wipe away every tear from their eyes. Death will be no more; mourning and crying and pain will be no more.

Such passages are inspiring and comforting. This is the most powerful medicine that the Christian owns. We pull it out at funerals because that's when it is needed most, when we encounter people teetering on the brink of despair. Such passages tell us that the Christian message is more than faith and love, that hope is absolutely crucial to all that we proclaim. I have come to believe that in order to understand the importance of hope in the Christian message, we need to understand the progression from what *could be* to what *is*: there are **wishes, hopes, faith,** and **knowledge.**

If a genie were to grant you one wish, what would you choose? If a genie would offer to grant you one *hope,* what would you choose? Is there any difference between those answers? Do you see any difference between wishes and hopes? If not, it's probably because our society tends to lump *wishes* together with *hopes.*

Furthermore, as I read and listen to political and religious discussions and ordinary conversation, it is apparent that many of us have a hard time telling the difference between *faith* and *knowledge.* More and more, what we are hearing from people is: "I believe it, so it's true." We act as if wishes = hope, and faith = knowledge. Actually, hope is much closer to faith than it is to a wish and faith is closer to hope than it is to knowledge. Here are four statements that illustrate the difference between these four states of being:

I *wish* the Minnesota Vikings would win a Super Bowl in my lifetime.

I *hope* that somebody gains something valuable by reading this book.

I *believe* in a loving God.

I *know* that 2 + 2 = 4.

Let's break that down:

I wish the Vikings would win a Super Bowl in my lifetime. A wish carries no expectation. I would very much like to see it happen, but I have no reason to think that I will ever see the Vikings win a Super Bowl. In fact, if it happens, I will be shocked.

I hope that somebody gains something valuable by reading this book. That carries some expectation. I have very little data to support this expectation. Hopes are not built on evidence. But I would not have bothered to write this book without some hope this would happen.

I believe in a loving God. I cannot prove the existence of a loving God. But my experience and understanding of the world makes me certain enough of this belief that I am willing to center my life on it. I can advocate for this faith but I cannot expect or insist that others accept it.

I know that 2 + 2 = 4. I can prove it through the use of logic and I can insist that others accept this as truth.

A wish is a desire.
Hope is a plea.
Faith is an opinion.
Knowledge is fact.

A wish is fantasy.
Hope is a prayer.
Faith is confidence.
Knowledge is certainty.

A wish says, "Wouldn't it be nice if…"
Hope says, "It has to be or I'm lost."
Faith says, "This is how it looks to me."
Knowledge says, "This is how it is and I can prove it."

Wishes are saturated with doubt.
Hope is surrounded by doubt.
Faith wrestles with doubt.
Knowledge erases doubt.

Wishes are blind.
Hope sees a little, and trusts a lot.
Faith sees a lot, and trusts almost as much.
Knowledge sees enough so that it requires no trust.

Why are hope and faith the most closely related of those four in the context of Christianity? Because of what or who they depend on.

Wishes depend on nothing. Most prayers I hear are not really prayers; they are wishes. It's fine to share our wishes with God. I do so frequently. My mother had severe dementia. For years, I wished with all my heart that she would wake up the next day knowing who I was, and that I could converse with her as I once did. I told that to God. But I had no illusions that this wish would come true, and it did not. God is not a genie. God does not deal in wishes.

Knowledge depends on facts. God is not a necessary part of that picture. We do not need God in order for us to accept facts.

Hope and faith, however, depend on God. The difference between the two is that with faith, God is at the center of a lot of things, including evidence and experience. *With hope, God is very close to being all there is.*

I don't think Christian leaders have done a good job of distinguishing between hope and faith. I often hear that whatever faith we have is a gift from the Holy Spirit. Here is my problem with that. If the Spirit is solely responsible for the creation of faith, it means that God chooses who believes and who does not. And if that is the case, then all this talk about saving and not being saved, and Jesus' statements about "great is your faith" are silly exercises. It's like taking credit for being tall. We have no part to play in any of this—we're just pawns in a pointless cosmic game.

But as we study the world, we find that God has created it to be understood and has given us the ability to understand it. Why? So that we would totally ignore all the evidence that God has enabled us to access, and simply believe whatever the Holy Spirit makes us believe? Or did God create the world with all its laws, resources, logic and rationality so that we would have a basis for determining what we believe?

There is a popular myth among the faithful that the best and most admirable religious people are those who hold tenaciously to faith regardless of all available evidence. If that were true, I would have to admire terrorists and cults.

I believe that God has given us experience and reason as tools for meeting God. Our faith is the result of interactions between the Holy Spirit, our experience of the world, our rational understanding, and our determination of who and what has proven reliable. Rather than saying that God determines who has faith, I would say that God has given us the means by which we come to faith.

But hope? That is different. Hope is a gift from God, pure and simple. It is something God gives freely to everyone, without exception. Hope is a promise from God, and to be honest, it is no more than a promise.

Hope is God's promise that life has meaning, that God's outpouring of love seeks out and finds all creatures in this world, even you, *especially you*. This gift of hope makes life possible, for without it, any meaning to life evaporates. Hebrews 11 describes the relationship between hope and faith like this: "Faith is the assurance of things hoped for, the conviction of things unseen." Faith springs from hope. When you begin to see evidence that the promises of God are reliable, that God is love, that your life has meaning, hope begins to grow into something called faith.

Faith takes over from hope.

That does not mean that hope disappears. That gift from God is always there when we need it. Since faith is partially dependent on what we do and what we think, and since we are imperfect creatures, there are times when faith weakens, or wavers, or crumbles, or even disappears. In times like that, hope takes over. Hope keeps us going until the pain or bitterness or emptiness or cynicism subsides enough so that the evidence for faith can reappear. Hebrews 6 describes hope as an unbreakable spiritual lifeline. "Hold on to it with both hands and never let it go," says verse 18. "Never let it go."

Elie Wiesel wrote hauntingly about his experience in the death camps of Nazi Germany in a book called *Night*. Most of the concentration camp victims, including Wiesel, lost their faith in God during that unspeakable nightmare. In such a setting, the evidence for belief simply was not there. The best that they could do in the midst of such overpowering evil was cling to hope. Not all those who held on to hope made it through those dark days. But Wiesel says that hope was the key to survival in the concentration camp. Every person who lost hope lost their spiritual lifeline and soon died. Only those who held onto hope survived.

In time, lost or wavering faith can return. In Wiesel's case it took several decades, while he clung to nothing but the thin thread of hope. But it finally returned, although certainly not in the exact form as it had been. As long as hope remains, faith can return.

Hope is there to catch us in the times when faith fails. In those moments when our faith is weak. When the evidence seems to say that faith is not possible. In times like that, hope is the thin lifeline that connects us to God.

Hope is a plea, begging God to be there.

Hope is a prayer to a God who may seem impossibly distant.

Hope is what keeps us afloat when the raging seas of doubt

wash away our faith.

Hope sees a little, trusts a lot.

Hope says, "It has to be this way or I'm lost."

The gospel of Jesus Christ is not proof of anything. There may be times when that story provides evidence for faith; times when it does not. What the Bible *always* does is awaken hope. Hope is the foundation of every future. For the Christian, everything that will come to pass is built on the message of hope that is best told in this story. That bond of hope between God and creation is the free gift that God gives to all people. It is a promise that wherever your future takes you, God will be there, whether you can feel that presence or not. It is the promise that the words of eternal life are true. That promise allows everything else to fall into place. It opens us up to the evidence that forms our faith.

We can live without wishes. By themselves, they do not impact our lives.

We can live without faith. Many agnostics and atheists do.

We can live without knowledge, as evidenced by any number of political movements and conspiracy theories.

But no one can live without hope.

Because of that, I would rank hope right behind love as the greatest gift God has given to humankind—even greater than the gift of faith.

Revelation says that God will wipe every tear from our eyes, and mourning and crying and pain will be no more. Thank God for this gift of hope. Hang on to it like a lifeline; grab it with both hands and never let go.

Chapter 28

I Wonder:
What happens to me when I die?

So this guy dies and he goes up to heaven and meets St. Peter at the pearly gates.

There are hundreds of jokes that have some form of that scenario in them. That's kind of the catch-all vision of heaven in our culture. The movie *Ghost* gives the standard corollary religious view of the end of life, when the screaming banshees arrive at the moment of death to whisk off the bad guy to the depths of despair, to the pits of hell, to pay for his crimes by roasting for all eternity.

Where do we get these views of a gated city in the clouds and Grim Reapers claiming their due? Is there any truth to any of it? The end of life is so fraught with uncertainty that even those with no religious interest at all can get lost in a kind of anxious wonder: What really happens to us when we die? What is heaven like? Will we be with our loved ones? What form will we have? Will we have any kind of a recognizable body? What age will we be? Will an elderly person ravaged by disease appear as the person they were when they were younger? Will a stillborn child have the personality she would have had, had she lived? What will heaven look like? What will we do there? Is there such a thing as purgatory, a celestial form of in-house detention for remedial Christians? Will there be a Judgment Day? Will our pets make it to heaven? Who's going to get to heaven and who won't? Is the whole idea of an afterlife all just a mirage?

Science is a gift we have been given to learn about God's creation, but science is of no help at all in dealing with these questions. Science, by definition, deals with this world and this world only, and even the occasional anecdotal evidence of near-death experiences does not carry much weight in the realm of science. Science has nothing to say about what happens after we die, other than in a straight physiological sense. So where do we go for answers?

There are only two places to which we can turn—our imaginations and our religious and spiritual resources.

Why is it that so many cultures have an afterlife ingrained in their teachings? The Elysian Fields, the River Styx, the halls of Valhalla, the celebratory gardens of Islam, heaven, and hell. Even the most secular people in the world speak, with tears in their eyes, about a loved one looking down on them, usually proudly, at a moment of achievement.

All this points to a strong, widely held belief that there is a life that occurs elsewhere after this one is over. In the absence of any possible scientific evidence, why do we believe this stuff? And how do we come to an understanding of what awaits us? How do we talk about something when we have no clear understanding of what it is and no access to any details? What are we to believe about something that lies beyond the limits of our imagination?

As Christians, we get our clues as to what happens to us after we die from the Bible. The Bible has a great deal to say about heaven and hell and eternal life. The trick, as always, is trying to figure out exactly what the Bible is saying. The only way the Bible or anyone can speak about eternal life is through metaphor. Metaphors are the only tool we have to say with any certainty what heaven is. When something is beyond our experience, when we cannot see it, experience it, or even describe it: all we can do is say it is in some way *like* something within our experience. It is not anything in our experience but parts of it are *like* some things in our experience.

Problems come when we try to turn metaphor into reality. For example, 1700 years ago, a monk was speculating about injustice and unfinished business at the end of our lives. He used his imagination to come up with an illustration or metaphor for this carryover of failure from this world into the next. He called it purgatory. Since this monk, Augustine, was widely respected, his words were read and studied. Pope Gregory, failing to understand what metaphor is, took Augustine's words as reality. In fact, his literal reading of a metaphor that is not even in the Bible became established church policy.

That happens more often than not with heaven. People have trouble coming to grips with the fact that every description of heaven in the Bible is metaphor. It has to be, because, by definition, an afterlife is not something we can experience in this world. The only way we can talk about things outside our experience is through metaphor.

How does the Bible do that? The Old Testament does it with poetry such as Psalm 14:2 "The Lord looks down from heaven on the sons of man to see if there are any who understand." There the Psalmist is using an image from his world view to describe the one thing that he knows to be true about heaven: it is a place where God is. Subsequent generations have taken that metaphor and misinterpreted it as reality—a reality that assumes the earth is flat, and is surrounded by a dome that separates the waters of the universe from the dry part of earth. If this is reality and not metaphor, then heaven is up there. Heaven is in the clouds.

Like all metaphors, it does not work as literal reality. Since our world is a sphere, the words "up" and "down" have no fixed meaning in the cosmos. Is God then looking up from heaven at Argentina or straight across from heaven at the Congo? If heaven is only up, how can God see anything in Australia?

Our society talks about going up to heaven, about our loved ones looking down on us from heaven. We talk about heaven being up, and hell being down. Useful as metaphors, not to be confused with reality.

Revelation presents a vision of heaven as being filled with strange, six-winged creatures, sort of a reprise of a vision in the Old Testament Book of Isaiah. Chapter 4, verse 8 of Revelation says, "Day and night they never stop saying: 'Holy, holy, holy is the Lord God Almighty who was, and is, and is to come.'" This inspired these words from a familiar hymn: "When we've been there 10,000 years, bright shining as the sun, we've no less days to sing God's praise, than when we've first begun."

This has proven to be a useful metaphor that helps us to see that eternal life sweeps away all selfishness and greed and provides us with pure relationship with God, the center of all life and love. Yet so many take it as literal fact, that heaven is a place where all we will do is sing praises to God. That does not sound real exciting to me, and I cannot imagine God would care much for that scenario. Useful as a metaphor, not to be confused with reality.

In Matthew 16, Jesus uses the metaphor of keys to the kingdom to help Peter see the responsibility he's been given. If you take that as reality, St. Peter is the guy standing at the gates of heaven determining who gets in and who does not. Revelation uses the metaphor of pearl gates to describe the beauty of heaven. Take that as reality, now you've got Peter standing at the pearly gates. By taking metaphor as reality, we have created a rather silly view of heaven, one that the Bible never intended. We forget the more important metaphor in those verses of Revelation; that the gates to heaven are never closed. Not only is St. Peter not guarding them—*no one* is guarding them.

The Bible offers many descriptions of heaven, all metaphors, none to be taken as reality. Revelation explains why in Jesus' declaration, "Behold, I am making all things new." The reality of afterlife is so far outside our experience that we cannot grasp the reality of it. My wife has described the transition to heaven in terms of the transition from womb to birth. Can any fetus in the womb have any clue what awaits them? Similarly, can anyone on earth have any idea what awaits them in an afterlife? All we have are metaphors to give us an idea of what it is *like*.

The Bible has two very simple points to make about heaven,

about the afterlife. I think C.S. Lewis made these points very well in the seventh and final book of his *Chronicles of Narnia*. Lewis painted a very vivid picture of heaven. He described running and not getting tired; he described racing up a waterfall. He described being bombarded by constant beauty. If you were to ask him what is the reality of heaven, Lewis would have been the first to tell you that there is not a word in his description that corresponds to reality. When Lewis entered eternal life, he would have been stunned if any of the specific details of his account were correct. His entire description is a metaphor that exists to tell us two things about heaven: It is being with God, and it is better than we can possibly imagine.

That is exactly what the Bible says about heaven. At the end of Revelation, John presents a flood of wonderful metaphors for heaven. So many people try to make a reality out of those metaphors. They try to use the book to piece together what is going to happen at the end of all times—the timeline, physical details.

But, like Lewis's work, all these metaphors exist to say two things. 1) The definition of heaven is being with God. Jesus says, "I am the Alpha and Omega. The beginning and the end." If you want to know what lies ahead at the end of all time, that's your answer. My seminary advisor, Dr. Craig Koester, teaches that the end, the Omega, is not a place, nor an event, nor a time. It is a person—the person of God, whom the Christian knows through Jesus Christ.

That is a restatement of what Jesus said in the Gospel of John, where he comes right out and gives an iron-clad definition of heaven. "Now this is eternal life," says Jesus. "That they may know you, the only true God, and Jesus Christ, whom you have sent."

Heaven is available to all. It is a free gift. The gates are open all the time. No one is guarding it. So why is heaven only for those who believe? Because nothing is true for you if you do not accept it. If you have no interest in being with God, that is your choice. If you have no interest in being with what you view as a fictitious construct of the human imagination, you will have created your own accommodation.

According to John, heaven is being with God, in this world and any world that comes. All that other stuff, the pearly gates, the mansion with many rooms, the New Jerusalem that rises in the heavens in a cube 1000 miles on each side, the river of crystal, that's all metaphor to say it will be great, beyond our ability to imagine it.

What is heaven? I have no clue. I can tell you nothing about it. All those questions about what form we take, and what we do, and are there pets and all that, I have no idea. For all the wondering that I do, I don't spend much time wondering about that, simply because it doesn't accomplish anything. There is no way to find out the details of an afterlife. It's all new. There's no data available from which to draw any conclusions.

What is heaven? I can tell you exactly what I believe it is. It is being with God. It is wonderful. That's all I can ever know.

CHRISTIAN ALTERNATIVE
BOOKS

THE NEW OPEN SPACES

Throughout the two thousand years of Christian tradition there
have been, and still are, groups and individuals that exist in
the margins and upon the edge of faith. But in Christianity's
contrapuntal history it has often been these outcasts and
pioneers that have forged contemporary orthodoxy out
of former radicalism as belief evolves to engage with and
encompass the ever-changing social and scientific realities. Real
faith lies not in the comfortable certainties of the Orthodox,
but somewhere in a half-glimpsed hinterland on the dirt track
to Emmaus, where the Death of God meets the Resurrection,
where the supernatural Christ meets the historical Jesus,
and where the revolution liberates both the oppressed and
the oppressors.

Welcome to Christian Alternative... a space at the edge where
the light shines through.
If you have enjoyed this book, why not tell other readers by
posting a review on your preferred book site.
Recent bestsellers from Christian Alternative are:

Bread Not Stones
The Autobiography of An Eventful Life
Una Kroll
The spiritual autobiography of a truly remarkable woman
and a history of the struggle for ordination in the Church of
England.
Paperback: 978-1-78279-804-0 ebook: 978-1-78279-805-7

The Quaker Way
A Rediscovery
Rex Ambler
Although fairly well known, Quakerism is not well understood.
The purpose of this book is to explain how Quakerism works as
a spiritual practice.
Paperback: 978-1-78099-657-8 ebook: 978-1-78099-658-5

Blue Sky God
The Evolution of Science and Christianity
Don MacGregor
Quantum consciousness, morphic fields and blue-sky
thinking about God and Jesus the Christ.
Paperback: 978-1-84694-937-1 ebook: 978-1-84694-938-8

Celtic Wheel of the Year
Tess Ward
An original and inspiring selection of prayers combining
Christian and Celtic Pagan traditions, and interweaving their
calendars into a single pattern of prayer for every morning
and night of the year.
Paperback: 978-1-90504-795-6

Christian Atheist
Belonging without Believing
Brian Mountford
Christian Atheists don't believe in God but miss him: especially the transcendent beauty of his music, language, ethics, and community.
Paperback: 978-1-84694-439-0 ebook: 978-1-84694-929-6

Compassion Or Apocalypse?
A Comprehensible Guide to the Thoughts of René Girard
James Warren
How René Girard changes the way we think about God and the Bible, and its relevance for our apocalypse-threatened world.
Paperback: 978-1-78279-073-0 ebook: 978-1-78279-072-3

Diary Of A Gay Priest
The Tightrope Walker
Rev. Dr. Malcolm Johnson
Full of anecdotes and amusing stories, but the Church is still a dangerous place for a gay priest.
Paperback: 978-1-78279-002-0 ebook: 978-1-78099-999-9

Do You Need God?
Exploring Different Paths to Spirituality Even For Atheists
Rory J.Q. Barnes
An unbiased guide to the building blocks of spiritual belief.
Paperback: 978-1-78279-380-9 ebook: 978-1-78279-379-3

Readers of ebooks can buy or view any of these bestsellers by clicking on the live link in the title. Most titles are published in paperback and as an ebook. Paperbacks are available in traditional bookshops. Both print and ebook formats are available online.

Find more titles and sign up to our readers' newsletter at
http://www.johnhuntpublishing.com/christianity
Follow us on Facebook at
https://www.facebook.com/ChristianAlternative